Women
in Traditional China

Ancient Times to Modern Reform

by
Susan Hill Gross & Marjorie Wall Bingham

Written under **Women In World Area Studies**, an ESEA, Title IV-C Federal Project granted by the Minnesota Department of Education.

Project Co-Directors: Marjorie Wall Bingham and Susan Hill Gross
Project Assistant: Nancy Keyt Wright

GEM
GARY McCUEN
publications inc.

411 Mallalieu Drive
Hudson, Wisconsin 54016

Photo Credits

Museum of Fine Arts, Boston 15
William Rockhill Nelson Gallery 17, 47a
BBC Hulton Picture Library 20
Gail Mathisen 22, 25, 28, 58, 80, 82
British Museum 27
Fratelli Fabri 47c
Richard Bancroft 77
China Reconstructs, June, 1974 9
Arthur Galston and Jean Savage, *Daily Life in People's China* (T.Y. Crowell), photo p. 68. Copyright © 1973 by Arthur W. Galston. Reprinted by permission of Harper & Row, Publishers, Inc. 84
Girl Rebel: The Autobiography of Hsieh Pingying, translated by Adet and Anor Lin (John Day). Copyright, 1940, by Harper & Row, Publishers, Inc., photo opposite p. 8. 5lb

Acknowledgments

Excerpts from *Under the Ancestors' Shadow* by Francis L. K. Hsu with the permission of the publishers, Stanford University Press. Copyright © 1948, 1967 by Francis L. K. Hsu.

Poems from *The Orchid Boat: Women Poets of China* by Kenneth Rexroth and Ling Chung. English translation copyright © 1972 by the authors. Used by permission of The Seabury Press, Inc.

Excerpts from *Courtier and Commoner in Ancient China: Selections from the History of the Former Han by Pan Ku,* translated by Bruce Watson, 1974. Reprinted with the permission of Columbia University Press.

Poems in Kai-yu Hsu's article "The Poems of Li Ch'ing-Chao," *PMLA,* 77 (1962), 521-528. Reprinted by permission of the Modern Language Association of America.

Excerpts from *A Chinese Village, Taiton, Shantung Province* by Martin Yang, 1945. Reprinted by permission of Columbia University Press.

Excerpts from *The Golden Wing* by Lin Yao-hua, 1948. Reprinted by permission of Routledge & Kegan Paul, Ltd.

Excerpts from *The House of Exile* by Nora Waln (Boston: Little, Brown and Company, 1933).

Excerpts reprinted from *Ruth V. Hemenway, M.D., A Memoir of Revolutionary China, 1924-1941,* edited with an introduction by Fred W. Drake (The University of Massachusetts Press, 1977), Copyright © 1977 by Fred W. Drake.

Excerpts from *Women and the Family in Rural Taiwan* by Margery Wolf, 1972. Reprinted by permission of the publisher, Stanford University Press.

Selection reprinted from *You Can Get There From Here* by Shirley MacLaine, by permission of W. W. Norton & Company, Inc. Copyright © 1975 by Shirley MacLaine.

"The Chinese Language Today: Romanization" from *China: Yesterday and Today,* Second Edition, edited by Molly Joel Coye and Jon Livingston. Copyright © 1975, 1979 by Bantam Books, Inc. Reprinted by permission of the publisher. All rights reserved.

Excerpts from *Pan Chao: Foremost Scholar of China* by Nancy Lee Swann, published by The Century Company, 1932. Reprinted by the permission of the Princeton University Library.

Selected abridged from pp. 18-19 in *Girl Rebel: The Autobiography of Hsieh Pingying,* translated by Adet and Anor Lin (John Day). Copyright, 1940, by Harper & Row, Publishers, Inc. Reprinted by permission of the publisher.

Excerpts from *A Daughter of Han* by Ida Pruitt, 1967. Reprinted by permission of Yale University Press.

Excerpts from *Daughter of Confucius* by Earl Herbert Cressy. Copyright 1952 by Earl Herbert Cressy. Reprinted by permission of Farrar, Straus and Giroux, Inc.

Women in World Cultures (Women in World Area Studies) is a project of St. Louis Park Independent School District #283 and Robbinsdale Independent School District #281, Title IV:C ESEA. The opinions and other contents of this book do not necessarily reflect the position or policy of the State of Minnesota or the U.S. Government and no official endorsement should be inferred.

Design, illustrations and typography by Richard Scales Advertising, Inc., Minneapolis, Minnesota.

publications inc.

411 Mallalieu Drive • Hudson, Wisconsin 54016
International Standard Book Numbers
0-86596-002-X Paper Edition
0-86596-027-5 Library Edition

Preface

The authors of *Women in Modern China* wish to acknowledge the special assistance of the following people in preparing this book:

Linda Walton-Vargo, area consultant
Ann Bailey, reader
Sally Hart, reader and language consultant
Nancy Slaughter, traveler's report
Richard Bancroft, photographs
Gail Mathisen, photographs
Hua-yuan Li Mowry, consultant
Rosemary Johnson, editor
Tom Egan, reader
Bert Gross, editor
Mike Cooley, pilot teacher
Tom Crampton, pilot teacher
Marjorie Ferris, pilot teacher
Jerry Gottstein, pilot teacher
Joel Tormoen, pilot teacher

In addition to these individuals, the University of Minnesota Library staff cooperated with time and patience to make research for this book possible.

Table of Contents

Introduction

WOMEN IN WORLD CULTURES is the product of a federally funded grant to develop materials on women for global studies and world history courses. The books are available in both hardback editions for library use and paper editions that may be purchased in sets of multiple copies for the classroom.

This project grew out of a search of resources which showed a clear lack of available materials appropriate for the study of women in other cultures. Women's roles in the history of various areas of the world were not included in usual curriculum and library materials. Women's lives were often subsumed under such titles as "the history of man," "the family," or "exceptional women." There were few attempts to explain or to describe how various classes of women lived at different times in particular cultures.

Cultural values were not analyzed in the context of the position of women. For example, Athens of the 5th century B.C. was usually called the "Golden Age" of Greece. Yet Athenian women had very restricted opportunities and diminished status compared to both earlier and later periods of Greek history. Materials that described Islam and the Arab world usually showed little understanding or acknowledgment of the powerful role that Muslim women often played within their "separate" worlds. In discounting the female half of humanity, the global curricular materials often seriously distorted the history and culture of these world areas.

WOMEN IN WORLD CULTURES has been designed to provide students with some resources for discovering the diversity of women's roles in a variety of world cultures. Each book presents both historical roles of women and information on their contemporary status. A major effort has been made to incorporate primary source materials. Descriptions by women of their own lives have been used whenever possible. Other types of information used include government reports, statistics, anthropologist's data, folklore, and art.

Each classroom unit includes a set of books, one teacher's guide and a sound filmstrip. A glossary of terms and a bibliography in each book aid students investigating an unfamiliar world area. The units are designed to supplement regular course offerings. The ones now available are: *Women in India, Women in the USSR, Women in Islam, Women in Israel, Women in Traditional China, Women in Modern China.* Future units include: *Women in Africa, Women in Latin America, Women in Ancient Greece and Rome, Women in Medieval and Renaissance Europe* and *Women in Modern Europe.*

Each unit has been field tested and revised to meet student and teacher comments. Students have been enthusiastic about the materials. Since these units are mainly centered around people's lives and emphasize social history, they are appealing to young people.

5

Chapter 1
Women in Ancient China

Chapter Contents

A. The Very Distant Past: A Pre-historic Chinese Matriarchy?

Chinese Communist historians generally accept a theory of history that says that Chinese society was originally a matriarchy,[1] run by women. To understand why they accept this idea, it is necessary to look briefly at 19th century historical philosophy.

In the mid-1800's a Swiss scholar, Johann Bachofen, published a collection of his works which he titled, *The Motherright*. At that time the ideas he presented in *The Motherright* were considered revolutionary and shocking. Until Bachofen, most scholars had assumed that from early times human families had been patriarchal -- meaning that the father was the dominant leader and the family name and inheritance passed through the male line. Bachofen presented a vast amount of evidence to indicate that human societies of the distant past had been *matriarchal* rather than patriarchal. During this matriarchal stage, family name and inheritance were passed down from the mothers of the families (matrilineal) and families were centered around the mothers' home (matrilocal). According to Bachofen, during this stage, women held the highest positions of respect. Female gods were most important and women were the rulers. It was only at a later stage of evolution that societies became patriarchal -- all societies had gone through this matriarchal stage first.

Bachofen's ideas attracted the attention of many social theorists. These included Karl Marx and Frederick Engels, the political philosophers whose writings are the basis of modern communism. They made the concept of a distant time of matriarchy a basic part of communist theory. According to this communist theory, the woman in the family is suppressed and dominated by the patriarchal male -- the way workers in a capitalist society are suppressed by the upper classes. Communism would get rid of both capitalism and patriarchy. According to Engels, "the overthrow of mother-right (or matriarchy) was the world historical defeat of the female sex."[2]

1. Matriarchy: where the mother is head of the household and descent lines are traced through the mother.
2. Frederick Engels, *The Origin of The Family, Private Property and the State* (New York: International Publishers, 1972), p. 120.

Many modern social scientists disagree with Bachofen's ideas. They do not deny that there is much evidence for matriarchies in the distant past and that some still exist today among small social groups. However, most modern anthropologists do not feel that all societies went through a matriarchial stage. But since communist theory accepts the idea of a matriarchial stage, most communist countries still are interested in finding evidence for a matriarchy in their past.

In 1973, the American film actress, Shirley MacLaine, was invited to tour China with a group of American women. Toward the end of the tour she journeyed 600 miles from Beijing[3] into the interior of China to Xian -- one of the ancient capitals of China. In Xian, MacLaine was taken to visit archaeological remains of an early civilization that her Chinese guides described as showing evidence of both a communistic life style and of the existence of a matriarchy in ancient China:

"...I visited the Banbo Museum, built in 1958 over the archaeological remains of a Chinese civilization that was 6000 years old.... These ruins had been unearthed six feet below the surface, and despite the age of the land and the ruins, the Chinese guides insisted on explaining that forgotten civilization in terms of Mao's [communist] China.

"They claimed that the civilization was communal, which might indeed have been true, but there was simply no visible evidence to support such a theory. I saw a deep ditch surrounding the ruins, to protect the inhabitants from wild animals, and there was a storage bin for human waste materials and garbage. The guides claimed the bin was communal, and therefore there were no social classes in ancient China. At death, each person was buried with three relics, and this was supposed to prove that there was no private ownership of goods.

"Each family obviously lived privately; even I could see that. And each home was separated from the next by a circular mound of earth. The guides told us that the Xian ruins were from a matriarchal society, in which women were the principal organizers because they were better acquainted with planting, farming, and other agricultural tasks, while their men hunted for meat. The surviving artifacts, which the guides said were made by women, were advanced and imaginative; birds and animals sculpted on clay, paintings made on the sides of homes, on pottery, shells, and bark, and there were a number of examples of bracelets and earrings, evidence of a society that had time for matters beyond mere survival."[4]

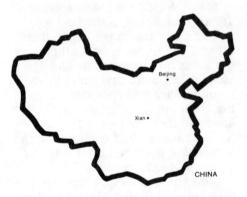

Beijing

Xian •

CHINA

3. Pinyin is used throughout *Women in Traditional China* except in the case of a few tribal or minority names. In the case of certain famous historical personages no attempt has been made to change the romanization of their names as it was felt such changes would create confusion rather than clarify pronunciation.
4. Shirley MacLaine, *You Can Get There from Here* (New York: W.W. Norton & Company, Inc., 1975), pp. 204–205.

Site of ancient Banbo Village at Xian.

Besides these communist interpretations of this site as an ancient matriarchy, some non-communist scholars of Chinese culture have also believed that women in pre-historic China may have had a dominant role. The most prominent of these was a French sociologist and China scholar, Marcel Granet, who wrote many important books on Chinese culture in the early part of the 20th century.

Granet particularly studied Chinese myths and early folk tales that he felt showed women in highly honored positions. Since the processes of fertility and reproduction were unclear to these ancient people, Granet felt that:

"...It was in fact a time when births were acquired at the sole profit of the wives and when the only reincarnations were those of maternal ancestors. It was the time when houses and villages belonged to the women. They ruled there, bearing the title of mothers... Earth itself appeared to be a Mother, giving fertility to women, and receiving it from them. Thus there was a period when the earth which had been inhabited and claimed had none but female attributes. Organization was then almost entirely matriarchal."[5]

5. Marcel Granet, *Chinese Civilization* (London: Kegan Paul, Trench, Trubner and Company, Ltd., 1930), pp. 171-172.

Whether either the Xian archaeological evidence or Granet's studies of ancient folk myths proves a matriarchy existed in ancient China is still open to question. It does appear that there is evidence that women in pre-historic China enjoyed high status. Later the status of women sharply declined from this high position.

Points To Consider

1. Why do you think Bachofen's theory of early matriarchies was considered "revolutionary and shocking" in the mid-1800's?

2. How did the communists see the issue of matriarchy vs. patriarchy? Why do communist countries still want to find a "matriarchy in their past"?

3. What makes MacLaine doubt that the people who had lived at the Xian site 6000 years ago were a communal society? What evidence is there at the site for its being a matriarchy? Does this seem like strong evidence to you? Why or why not?

4. Why might the fact that ancient people did not understand very well the fertility or reproduction processes contribute to the high status of women in ancient times?

B. Lady Li Zang: Autopsy of a 2000-year-old Woman

In 1972 archaelogists uncovered a tomb near Changsha in central China dating from the Former Han Dynasty (206 B.C. - 24 A.D.). It was an important find for archaeologists because the tomb contained pottery, clothing and other artifacts of artistic and historic value. Of even more scientific interest was the body of the woman buried in the tomb. From inscriptions on the tomb, it was discovered that the body was that of Lady Li, the wife of a minor Han official, the Marquis of Dai. Lady Li had died at the age of fifty. Her body had been wrapped in silk, and then been placed in an air-tight coffin inside a series of six boxes. Five tons of charcoal surrounded the boxes and coffin, which was then covered by a layer of white clay. This elaborate coffin was buried in 60 feet of earth. Inside the innermost coffin-box scientists discovered a mildly acid, reddish fluid that had helped to preserve the body.

Because of the complicated and complete embalming processes used to preserve the body, the state of preservation was remarkably good. For example, the skin of the body was soft -- unlike the dry skin of an Egyptian mummy. The hair was still tightly attached to the scalp and the joints of the body were flexible.

Chinese doctors performed an autopsy on the body as might be done for a recent death. They were able to determine that Lady Li had:[1]

--- borne children
--- at sometime suffered a broken forearm
--- spots on her lungs that showed that she had once had tuberculosis
--- several gallstones which were discovered in her gall bladder
--- eaten melons shortly before her death
--- a coronary artery almost closed by arteriosclerosis -- so the probable cause of death was a sudden heart attack (no bed sores were found on the skin which might have indicated a long illness)

1. Information on the discovery of the tomb and autopsy from: "The 2000 Year-Old Woman," *Time Magazine* (September 17, 1973), p. 55.

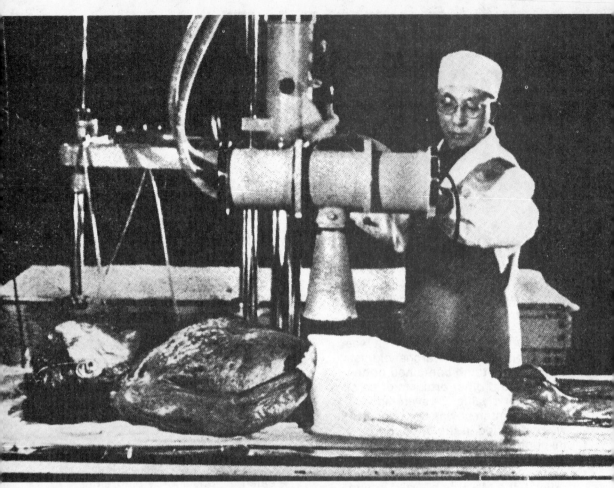

Autopsy of the corpse of Lady Li Zang.

Points To Consider

The discovery of Lady Li's tomb and body was of great scientific interest because of the remarkable preservation of the body. Doctors were excited to be able to perform a normal, modern autopsy on this 2000-year-old corpse. Although the results make a fascinating story, for historians of women there is another point of interest beyond the artistic and scientific evidence found in the tomb. Acting as historians, how would you tentatively answer the following questions that could be asked about the find of Lady Li's tomb?

1. What things might this elaborate tomb possibly indicate about the relationship of Lady Li and her husband, the Marquis of Dai?

2. What might the tomb and body indicate about women in general at the time of the Former Western Han Dynasty?

3. Why might generalizations about women in the Former Han Dynasty, made from the evidence of Lady Li's tomb, be open to question?

C. The Ideal Chinese Woman

During the Han Dynasty Liu Hsiang[1] wrote down stories and sayings that later became the "ideal" toward which Chinese women were supposed to strive. These "ideals" were not always accepted by Chinese women, but his book became a sort of textbook of Confucian[2] principles for women.

After each item, write a few words on your worksheet which seem to describe the characteristic for women which is stressed:

1. A woman came from a wealthy family, but dressed simply so that she could match the poverty level of her husband.

2. A man was caught by bandits in a famine period. They threatened to eat him, but his wife said she would die in his place. The bandits then ate her.

3. A woman was extremely nice to her sister-in-law and also obeyed her mother-in-law in whatever she wanted. The good example of this woman made the household live in harmony.

4. A man in the fields was attacked by a tiger. His daughter jumped on the tiger and beat it with her fists until it ran away.

5. Husbands and wives were not supposed to sit together, nor should their hands touch when giving or taking things.

6. The house of a widow was on fire. But when people urged her to escape, she refused because she could not respectably leave the house without a chaperone. She died in the flames.

7. A family tried to force a widow to remarry. She shaved her head, next cut off her ears and finally cut off her nose so that no one would want to marry her.

8. Mencius (a famous Chinese philosopher) played around in school until his mother lectured him. He then settled down and became a great scholar.

9. "A woman's place is in the kitchen. The affairs of government do not concern her."

10. When her mother was sick and wanted fish to eat in winter, a daughter went out and lay on the ice until it melted. Then she caught three fish and her mother quickly recovered.

1. Selections are from A. C. Safford (Trans.) Liu Hsiang's *Typical Women of China* (Shanghai: Kelly & Walsh, 1899).
2. A Chinese philosopher who lived in the 6th – 5th centuries B.C. and whose ideas became the basis of the Chinese social system.

Daughter saves Father from tiger.

Points To Consider

1. After looking over the characteristics described in these items, what would you say the "ideal" woman was supposed to be like?

2. Do any of the characteristics seem to contradict each other?

3. Which of the items do you think readers might find believable? Which not?

14

Women making silk

Chapter 2

Women in Historical China

Chapter Contents

16

A. The Empress and Empress Dowagers

Empress holding lotus blossom, Buddhism's sacred flower.

According to Confucian ideals, women had a subordinate position to men. Therefore, for a woman to rule China would upset the "natural order" of events. It would be, writers claimed, like a hen crowing at dawn. Traditional Chinese historians did mention a few women who had some power. But Confucian historians generally claimed these rulers were devious women who proved by their cruelty how terrible it was to let a woman have power. Recent scholarship has suggested, however, that women actually ruled China for a good deal of its history and that the women who had power used it in much the same way as the male emperors -- sometimes for the good of the country, sometimes not. The following list suggests some of the eras of empress control, either as regents or through their own influence:

17

Empresses Who Ruled

Approximate Date of Reign	Dynasty	Empress Dowager
194 B.C.	Han	Luzhi
105–121 A.D.	Han	Deng
132	Han	Liang
167	Han	He
188	Han	Dou
c. 195 B.C.	Han	Lu
442	Northern Wei	Wen-ing
465–471	Northern Wei	Feng
525–528	Northern Wei	Ling
589	Sui	Yang Jian
684–705	Chou	Wu
924	Liao	Ying dian
986	Liao	Cheng dian
1022–1033	Sung	Liu
1031	Liao	Chin
1085–1094	Sung	Gao
1079	Sung	Cao
1100	Sung	Xiang
1300	Ming	Ming yuan
1651–1667	Ching	Xiao zhuang
1860–1900 Co-regents	Ching	An Ci
1860–1908	Ching	Ci Xi

The way in which women obtained power was primarily through the position of "empress dowager." This position was that of mother to the current emperor, although sometimes the emperor might be her adopted son.

Theoretically, the empress dowager was only in charge of the women in the imperial court, setting up court etiquette, determining social events and generally seeing that life moved smoothly for the emperor, her son. However, her position had two other potential advantages that might give her power. One was that if the emperor were a true follower of Confucius, he owed "filial piety" to her. He had to listen to her advice and honor her; for example, the choice of his wife and his official concubines were generally his mother's decision, not his. Her second advantage was that she was part of the "Inner Court" and could often control the political events surrounding the emperor. For example, if she had strong control over her son, she might, like Empress Lu and Empress Ci Xi, kill off any children born to him and his wives. In that way, she might always pick a weak adopted son to continue her own power.

The position of emperor was a very powerful one throughout Chinese history, but it was also one that required a delicate sense of political balance. The emperor's position might be shown by the following diagram:

OUTER COURT
Government Officials
Governors
Generals

INNER COURT
Empress Dowagers
Empress, Concubines
Eunuchs

△
Emperor

Like a teeter totter, if either side got too much power, the nation's balance was lost. Often when this balance was lost, and the sides moved up and down in internal dispute, the foreign conquerors would move in. Sometimes the empress dowagers tried to bolster up the power of the emperor, as for example Empress Dowager Xiao Zhuang who taught her grandson Kang Xi well. Sometimes, however, as with the Empress Wu, the goal was to attain power by upsetting the emperor.

Whether or not the empress would be merely an official of the court or have real political power depended on a variety of factors. The following were often reasons for the taking of power by an empress either as an official regent or by acting behind the scenes:

1. *If the Emperor were young at the time of his coming to reign.*

   An historian has pointed out that the average life span of a Chinese Emperor was 39 years.[1] This meant that the emperor often did not have grown sons to follow him. Therefore, until the son was able to govern, his mother would be appointed regent. (Empresses Dou, Deng, Liang and Ci Xi would be examples of such appointments.[2])

Drawing of Empress Wu.

2. *If the Emperor became sick or incapable or ruling.*

   Empress Cao, for example, made decisions temporarily for her son. Empress Luzhi was asked to depose a poor ruler and several Ming empresses were called on to try to stop their sons' "debaucheries." Sometimes, however, mothers seemed to have encouraged their sons' wild ways, as did Empress Ci Xi and Empress Wu, to keep them occupied while the empresses ruled.

1. Wang Jiayou, *Loves and Lives of Chinese Emperors* (Taipei, Taiwan: MeiYa Publishers, 1972), p. 2.
2. Yang Liansheng, "Female Rulers in Imperial China," *Harvard Journal of Asiatic Studies*, XXIII, (1960–61), p. 51.

大清國慈禧皇太后

Empress Dowager Ci Xi.

3. If the Empress came from a powerful family.

The Chinese had something of a dilemma when it came to deciding what sort of person an empress might be. On the one hand, she should be educated, politically smart and well trained in etiquette -- a "lady," therefore, from a high status family. But on the other hand, if she came from too powerful a family, the family might take over. The two sister empresses Liang, for example, had their family made the real rulers of China.[3] Other empresses, like Empresses Wu, Ling and Lu, also relied on family support and made fortunes for their families.

4. If the Empress had connections with military power.

If the empress had some general to back her commands, her power was often assured. Some of the empresses, like Empress Liang, had relatives controlling the army. Some had lovers in the military; one of Empress Ci Xi's commanders, Rung Luo, saved her reign against both Manchu princes and later the Emperor himself. Among the Khitan empresses, like Ying tien and Qing Ai, were some who commanded their own armies and military camps.[4]

5. If the Empress came from Northern China.

Generally, there seems to have been more of an acceptance of women's participation in politics in North China. Perhaps this was because of the various tribal groups who seemed to believe in more open roles for women than did the "traditional" Chinese. Empress Ling of the Northern Wei, for example, was not confined to an "inner court," but traveled and took part in public ceremonies.[5]

6. If the Empress did not accept Confucianism.

Outside of "filial piety," the philosophy of Confucius did not have much to offer a woman who was interested in power. Other religions, like Buddhism, seemed to offer women more of a chance at spiritual equality and the female god of mercy, Guan Yin was a model for a kind, benevolent female ruler. The empresses Wu, Ci Xi and Ling were particularly known as supporters of Buddhism. Ci Xi even liked to be called "Old Buddha" and had herself painted as the god Guan Yin.

Other religions, the shamanism of the Manchu or Daoist beliefs, were also more accepting of women's ruling. One of the strong empress dowagers of the Manchus, Xiao Zhuang, was said to have been a Christian. These other faiths may have sustained the strong empresses against the Confucian charge that they were upsetting the "natural order" of rule.

7. If the Emperor's "face" needed saving.

As the Emperor was considered to be the Son of Heaven, it would be embarrassing to have him admit to weakness. The Empress was, for example, sent to ask for mercy from invaders. Also, the person who promulgated (handed out) the last emperor's notice of abdication was the Empress Yong Lu in 1912.[6]

3. Rafede Crespigny, "The Harem of Emperor Huan: A Study of Court Politics in the Latter Han," *Papers on Far Eastern History*, Vol. 12, (September, 1975), pp. 1–42.
4. Karl Wittfogel and Feng Jiasheng, *History of Chinese Society: Liao (907-1125)* (Philadelphia: The American Philosophical Society, 1949), p. 200.
5. Jennifer Holmgren, "Empress Dowager Ling of the Northern Wei and the Touba Sinicization Question," *Papers on Far Eastern History*, Vol. 18. (September, 1978), pp. 123–170.
6. Frank Dorn, *The Forbidden City* (New York: Charles Scribners, 1970), pp. 187–188.

The Marble Boat at the Summer Palace.

Once in power, what sort of rulers were these women? Almost any general history of China, written by the Chinese or by Westerners, seems to present the empress dowagers as: cruel, power-hungry, and extravagant. Usually, only two empresses, Empress Wu and Empress Ci Xi, are written about extensively to give proof for this stereotype. As new scholarship has appeared, however, a more complex picture appears.

It is true that some empress dowagers were cruel. The Empress Lu, for example, poisoned her son's rival and had his mother slowly sliced into pieces.[7] Empress Ci Xi forced her pregnant daughter-in-law to commit suicide, approved the drowning of the emperor's concubine, and probably had the emperor himself poisoned. Empress Wu is accused of executing 5000 members of the Tang family so that her family could take over and form a new dynasty.[8] These women were cruel. Whether they were unusually

7. Eloise Talcott Hibbert, *Embroidered Gauze* (London: John Lane, 1938), p. 85.
8. *Ibid.*, p. 165.

cruel compared to other emperors of their time is, however, difficult to gauge.

The three empresses listed above were, it is true, extravagant. Empress Wu built elaborate Buddhist temples. Perhaps the best known criticism of an empress' extravagance is against Ci Xi who spent money that should have gone to the Chinese navy on an elaborate Marble Boat for her Summer Palace.[9] Chinese emperors were also known for their extravagances, for example, the elaborate palaces built by the Manchus -- later burned by the British.

Yet, the question remains -- if these women at their worst were cruel and extravagant, why did they remain in power after they obtained it? In the case of these three, historians generally agree that they managed to hold China together at crucial times. Empresses Lu and Wu seemed even to have fairly peaceful reigns which benefited the general population.

But not all of the dowagers were known for their cruelty. One particularly influential empress dowager was Xiao Zhuang, mother of one emperor and grandmother of one of the best of the Manchu rulers, Kang Xi.[10] She raised her son in as moral and proper (some say dull) an atmosphere as possible. She forbade Chinese concubines from coming into the court and saw to it that her son was well educated. Though later she and her son disagreed, she took charge of her grandson's upbringing also. This emperor, Kang Xi, was known for his literary ability and acquaintance with Western education. He also had strong affection and respect for his grandmother as he himself described when writing about her death:

"...Now, as she lay in her coma, I had every kind of food prepared though she could eat none, every medicine ready, and I lay on a mat beside the bed listening for the slightest sound from her. When she died I had been near her side for thirty-five days and nights, never undressing, almost never sleeping, preparing her medicines, trying to anticipate her needs-- so that whether she wanted to lie or sit, eat or drink, nothing would be lacking. I had thirty kinds of rice gruel prepared, in the hopes of rousing her failing appetite. She patted my back, and cried...."[11]

Sometimes the sons seem to have gone to rather odd extremes to honor the empresses. To celebrate the Empress Dowager's 60th birthday in January, 1752, for example, Qianlong had the following done:[12]

--- Furnished the city of Beijing with silk decorations and lanterns
--- Placed artificial trees and flowers throughout the palace grounds
--- Had children dressed as monkeys and birds play on the grounds
--- Built new barges for the river
--- Tried by having thousands of Chinese beating the water to keep the ice from closing the river. (They failed.)
--- Brought 100 old men from throughout the country, each 100 years old. All were dressed alike and bearded when they gave special homage to the Empress.

9. Some of her defenders claim, however, that the Chinese military being what it was around 1900, full of corruption and inept commanders, the Marble Boat may have been a more long lasting investment.

10. Robert Oxnam, *Ruling from Horseback: Manchu Politics in the Oboi Regency 1661-1669* (Chicago: University of Chicago Press, 1975), pp. 167-203.

11. Jonathan Spence, *Emperor of China: Self Portrait of Kang Xi* (New York: Alfred Knopf, 1974), pp. 104-105.

12. Hope Danby, *The Garden of Perfect Brightness* (London: Williams and Norgate, 1950), pp. 129-132.

Another empress dowager who received respect was Empress Deng of the Latter Han Dynasty. She was praised for many achievements, among them:[13]

  --- cutting back on the budget
  --- not promoting her own family
  --- starting an imperial court school for both girls and boys
  --- providing grain to the poor in time of famine
  --- being a model of a well-educated, virtuous woman
  --- investigating her legal officials and releasing some innocent men

Other empresses, like the mothers of Prince Chani (Han Dynasty), Hai Shu (Chin Dynasty) and Sheng Zong (Ming Dynasty) were known to be wiser politically than their sons.

But even when the empress dowagers were respected, their lives were not necessarily easy. Perhaps one reason that the empress dowagers had a reputation for cruelty was that their position was an unsure one. The empress feared rival concubines and their ambitions for their own sons. The empress might also fear her husband's or son's lack of loyalty. Then there were also the eunuchs of the court who had to be bribed and kept loyal to her. If the empress over-reached her power and failed, her fate or her family's was often a brutal one. After the Empress Lu's death, for example, the army killed off every man, woman and child bearing the name of Lu.[14] Empress Cian and Empress Xu were poisoned. The Empress Wei and her family were killed when she tried to take power.[15]

Besides the possibility of a violent death that awaited the ambitious empress, there were other deterrents to women taking power. In the Northern Wei in 366-408 A.D., for example, an emperor tried to start the practice of killing the emperor's mother so that she could not gain power. But it seemed that another woman of the court would just step into the role, so the practice was abandoned.[16] Confucian historians tried to point out to later generations the misfortune of women ruling. Various imperial decrees were passed, as in 222 A.D. and 422, that the power of the empress dowager should be limited. In 1368 an emperor of the Ming Dynasty declared:

"...Although the empresses and imperial concubines should serve as models of mothers in the empire, they are not to be permitted to take part in government affairs."[17]

Yet, whatever the criticisms or decrees, the empress dowagers continued to play major roles in Chinese history. Whether that role was of benefit or harm to China was dependent often on the personality of the empress herself. But the record of the empresses seems to be more complicated than the stereotype of an evil, power-mad woman.

13. Nancy Lee Swann, "Biography of the Empress Deng," *Journal of the American Oriental Society*, Vol. 51 (1931), pp. 138–159.
14. Hibbert, p. 93.
15. Howard Levy, *Harem Favorites of an Illustrious Celestial* (Taiwan: Chung Tai Printing, 1958), p. 12.
16. Wang, p. 74
17. Yang, p. 52.

Bridge at the Imperial Summer Palace. Palace women who were isolated from society could walk in these gardens.

Points To Consider

1. Historians in traditional China would probably have gained their education and positions by being part of the Confucian system of examinations. Why might these historians have a particular bias when writing down events concerning empresses? How might that bias affect later historians?

2. Of the seven conditions which might make it possible for an empress to take power, which seem most important to you?

3. In what ways does the stereotype of the cruel empress dowager appear to be true? In what ways exaggeration?

4. Considering the risks, why would any woman want to become a powerful empress dowager?

B. The Imperial Concubines

Ancient Chinese historians sometimes had difficulties describing the "beneficial" reigns, and the "immoral" characters of some of empress dowagers. But they had less trouble deciding about the imperial concubines. The descriptions of these women seem to fall into two categories:

1) they were evil, pleasure-loving and ruined the emperor, or
2) they were refined and good, and only aided the emperor.

Either way, however, the fate of the concubine described usually ended tragically. Before examining the lives of some of these women perhaps an explanation is needed of the roles of an imperial concubine.

Generally, in China, a man was allowed to marry one wife, but he might also have secondary wives, concubines. While these women did not have all the rights and powers over the household as the first wife, their position in the household was recognized and their children considered as part of the family. Emperors usually had one empress as a wife, but there were various degrees of concubines below her authority. Sometimes, as in the case of the last important empress, Ci Xi, a woman might enter the court as a third degree concubine and, with the birth of a son, become the Empress Dowager. Though the future empress was chosen with some care -- her official duties meant she had to be fairly bright and well-educated -- the concubines were not always so strictly chosen. Sometimes, as in Ci Xi's case, an official was struck by her beauty even in the midst of her humble house. He sent her to the court where she was educated and later became an imperial concubine.[1]

During some periods in Chinese history, officials went through the countryside and brought good-looking women to the court for the emperor and his mother to choose for concubines. During the Manchu reign, young Manchu girls had to be registered with the Palace and every three years certain ones would be called to Beijing for inspection. If they passed, they would be ranked and would receive further education. Though some of the Chinese historians make it sound as if being an imperial concubine was a great honor, not everyone wanted to be chosen.[2]

First of all, the concubine, at least in Manchu days, was separated from her family who might only see her again on rare visits. Second, being chosen as a concubine did not necessarily mean that the woman would ever even meet the emperor. At the height of the Ming Dynasty, for example, it was estimated that

1. Eloise Hibbert, *Embroidered Gauze* (London: John Lane, 1938), p. 66.
2. In ancient China there seemed also to be a custom of killing and burning the concubines when the emperor died. The exact history of this custom is somewhat unclear.

Emperor and Concubines

there were 9,000 concubines at court; in the Qing Dynasty, 12,000.[3] Getting a chance to meet the emperor -- let alone impress him -- was often random chance. Bribery of eunuchs or the empress dowager sometimes helped arrangements. Concubines like Chao Chun who did not provide bribes, were sometimes overlooked.[4] Third, even if the concubine met the emperor and had his son, she would be subject to court jealousies. The poisonings, forced abortions and suicides of court concubines did not encourage parents who loved their daughters to register for "the emperor's choice." The last powerful empress dowager, Ci Xi, for example, had such a terrible reputation that one year no Manchu families registered their daughters.[5] One Manchu mother and father not only did not register their two daughters, but sent them to Europe in 1900 to study so that they would be safe.[6] In other periods parents tried to protect their

3. Lucian Pye, *China: An Introduction* (Boston: Little Brown & Company, 1972), p. 60.
4. Shu Chiung, *Chao Chun: Beauty in Exile* (Shanghai: Kelly & Walsh, 1934), pp. 33-36.
5. Harry Hussy, *Venerable Ancestor* (Garden City: Doubleday, 1949), p. 248.
6. Princess der Ling, *Kowtow* (New York: Dodd, Mead, 1929), pp. 88-95.

28   **The walkway where women strolled at the imperial summer palace.**

daughters by marrying them off early or by making them appear as ugly as possible. For poorer, more ambitious families, however, the daughter might be encouraged to take the risk for possible benefits, money and power, which could come to an emperor's favorite.

Once the concubine got the emperor's attention, her days would still be spent largely with the empress dowager and other court ladies. The emperor would, however, choose the tablet of the concubine he wished to see in the evening. She would be undressed completely by her maids, covered with a yellow robe, and then carried to the emperor's bed by a eunuch. The nudity of the concubine was more for defense than erotic purposes -- there was a fear that a concubine might kill the emperor.

After the eunuch was notified that he might carry the concubine back, the emperor was also asked if he wanted the concubine to bear his child. If not, contraceptive washing was done.[7] If he did wish a child, records of the date were kept to ensure the legitimacy of any sons.

Though the system of court life was rigid, the concubine was often the person of most emotional importance to the emperor. His mother, the empress dowager, might have political plans of her own, his wife had been chosen for him and his sons were potential rivals. His favorite concubine, then, might be the only person for whom he had affection, and he might reward that affection lavishly. Perhaps the contrast between the risks and benefits of a concubine's life is what attracted so many traditional Chinese authors to write plays, poems and stories about these imperial concubines. In the process of writing about them, however, the authors seem to fit them into either evil or good categories and it is difficult to understand what the real women

may have been like. Yet, all of them are seen as beautiful and tragic.

Here, very briefly, are some of the concubines who became noted in Chinese history:

The Evil Ones

A. (c. 1766 B.C.) *Daji*: She was beautiful, cruel and decadent. She and the emperor filled up a pool with liquor and they and their friends rowed about in small boats. Then, they jumped in and everyone got drunk.[8]

B. (c. 1122 B.C.) *Ta Ji*: She was so cruel she loved to watch torture. To settle an argument about who had more marrow in their bones, young men or old, she had men's bones broken and examined.

C. (c. 770 B.C.) *Baosi*: She was frivolous as well as cruel. She had the emperor light all the mountain watch fires just for fun. These fires were supposed to signal troops to come to aid the emperor. The troops were so disgusted at the "joke" they did not show up the next time the fires were lit. The emperor and she were defeated by actual enemies then.

D. (c. 730's A.D.) *Yang Guifei*: She was so extremely beautiful that the emperor devoted himself entirely to her and gave her sisters elaborate gifts. Their extravagance ruined the countryside and a rebellion threatened the emperor. She hanged herself as the army arrived.[9]

7. Taisuke Mitamura, *Chinese Eunuchs* (Rutland, Vt.: Charles Tuttle, 1970), pp. 112–113.
8. F. I. Hawks Pott, *A Sketch of Chinese History* (Shanghai: Kelly & Walsh, 1903), pp. 112–113.
9. Shu Jiong, *The Most Famous Beauty of China* (New York: D. Appleton & Co., 1924).

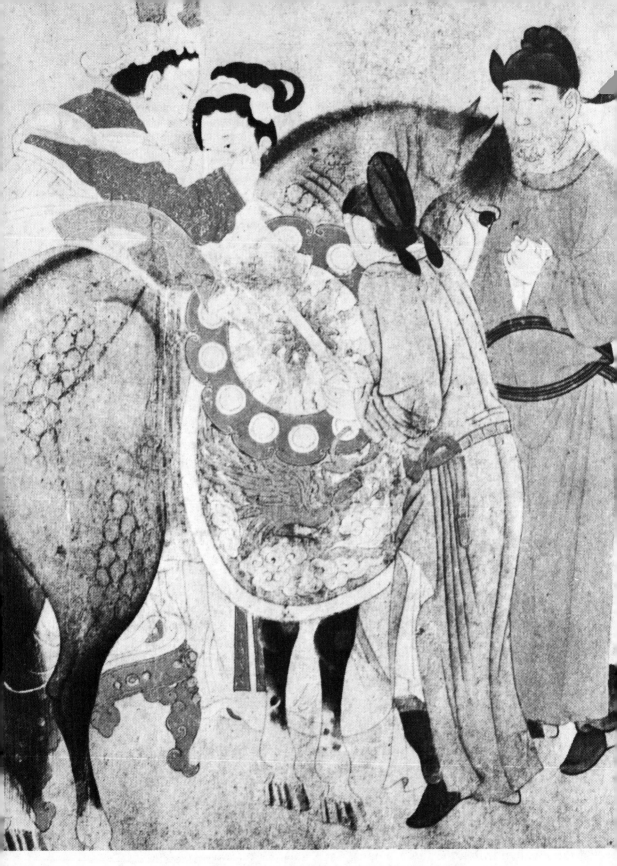

The concubine, Yang Guifei, mounting her horse.

The Good Ones

A. (c. 1 A.D.?) *Zhao Zhun*: She was beautiful, but neglected by the emperor because she did not bribe officials. She was married off to a Tartar Khan as part of the Chinese attempt to better relations with the barbarians. The Chinese emperor saw her as she left and was heartbroken at her beauty. Zhao was a good diplomat and kept her Tartar clan loyal to China, though she lived a harsh life away from the court. Her dying wish was to be buried in China; her grave (still a tourist attraction in the 1930's) was said to be evergreen.[10]

B. (c. 500 B.C.) *Xi Shi*: She was very loyal to her country and was educated for devious purposes. She was sent to the Emperor of Wu by his enemies to seduce him into a life of pleasure. When the treasury was empty, the enemies moved against Wu.[11] But even though she betrayed the leader of Wu, she felt some respect for him. She then jumped in a river and disappeared.[12]

C. (c. 1750's A.D.) *Fragrant Princess Xiang Fei*: She received her title because she seemed to have her own smell that drove men crazy with passion. She was originally from Central Asia; her husband was killed and she was sent as a prize to the Chinese emperor. She refused his attentions even though he was deeply in love with her. He built a model town in the Central Asian tradition so she would not be lonesome, and even had a Muslim mosque built for her religion. He spent so much time thinking about her that the empress dowager asked that she kill herself -- which she did. The Chinese particularly admire her as a virtuous widow.[13]

D. (c. 1900 A.D.) *Pearl Concubine*: She was loyal to the emperor who was controlled by Ci Xi, "Old Buddha," and tried to oppose this empress dowager. She seems to have been in favor, as the emperor was, of some reforms for China. When the Pearl Concubine protested against the emperor's not being able to rule, the empress dowager had her thrown into a well and drowned.[14]

None of these women wrote their own stories, and sometimes these women appear more like figures from a drama, good or evil, than as real people. Occasionally in the histories, we do get a glimpse of an individual concubine concerned about her fading beauty but ambitious for her family:

"...when Madam Li lay critically ill, the emperor came in person to inquire how she was, but she pulled the covers over her face and, apologizing, said 'I have been sick in bed for a long time and my face is thin and wasted. I cannot let Your Majesty see me, though I hope you will be good enough to look after my son the king and my brothers.'

"'I know you've been very sick, and the time may come when you never rise again,' said the emperor. 'Wouldn't you feel better if you saw me once more and asked me face to face to take care of the king and your brothers?'

10. Shu, *Zhao Zhun*, p. 168.
11. Shu Jiong, *Xi Shi, Beauty of Beauties* (Shanghai: Kelly & Walsh, 1931), p. 85.
12. Hibbert, p. 66.
13. *Ibid.*, pp. 253–269.
14. Princess der Ling, *Old Buddha* (New York: Dodd, Mead & Company, 1928), pp. 272–273.

"'A woman should not appear before her lord or her father when her face is not properly made up,' she said. 'I would not dare let Your Majesty see me in this state of disarray.'

"'Just let me have one glimpse of you,' said the emperor. 'I'll reward you with a thousand pieces of gold and assign your brothers to high office!'

"But Madam Li replied, 'It is up to Your Majesty to assign offices as you please-- it does not depend on one glimpse of me.'

"When the emperor continued to insist on one last look at her, Madam Li, sobbing, turned her face toward the wall and would not speak again. The emperor rose from his seat in displeasure and left.

"Madam Li's sisters berated her, saying, 'Why couldn't you let him have one look at you and entreat him face to face to take care of your brothers! Why should you anger him like this!'

"'The reason I didn't want the emperor to see me,' she said, 'was so I could make certain he would look after my brothers! It was because he liked my looks that I was able to rise from a lowly position and enjoy the love and favor of the ruler. But if one has been taken into service because of one's beauty then when beauty fades, love will wane, and when love wanes, kindness will be forgotten. The emperor thinks fondly and tenderly of me because he remembers the way I used to look. Now if he were to see me thin and wasted, with all the old beauty gone from my face, he would be filled with loathing and disgust and would do his best to put me out of his mind. Then what hope would there be that he would ever think kindly of me again and remember to take pity on my brothers?'

"When Madam Li died, the emperor had her buried with the honors appropriate to an empress. After that, he made her eldest brother Li Guangli, the Sutrishna general, as marquis of Maixi, and appointed her brother Li Yan xian as a chief commandant with the title "Harmonizer of the Tones."'[15]

The last of the imperial concubines probably died around the 1920's. But poetry and plays about them form a major part of traditional Chinese literature. For example, writing about Yang Guifei, Li Taibo described some of the romantic appeal of the beauty of the concubine soon to fade and die:

"What matter if the snow
Beat out the garden? She shall still lean
Upon the scented balustrade and glow
With spring that thrills her warm blood into wine."[16]

15. Burton Watson (Trans.), *Courtier and Commoner in Ancient China: Selections from the History of the Former Han by Pan Ku* (New York: Columbia University Press, 1974), pp. 248–249.
16. As quoted in Hibbert, p. 174.

Points To Consider

1. What were the advantages of being an imperial concubine?

2. For the "evil" concubines, what qualities did the Chinese seem to write about as being "evil"? What qualities were seen as being "good" in the "good" concubines?

3. One historian claims that the emperors spent 400,000 taels for cosmetics alone for court women. The expenses of keeping hundreds of concubines must have been enormous, and certainly court jealousies and rivalries led to problems. Also, a whole system of eunuchs was necessary to "protect" the women and that system became corrupt and costly. Why then do you think the system lasted as long as it did? (Might consider: prestige, foreign policy, making sure of heirs, greed?)

4. Why did the concubine refuse to let the emperor see her when she was dying? Do you think her view of human nature -- choosing beauty over affection -- is justified?

C. The Educated Woman

*"ON A VISIT TO CHONG ZHEN
TAOIST TEMPLE I SEE IN THE
SOUTH HALL THE LIST OF
SUCCESSFUL CANDIDATES IN
THE IMPERIAL EXAMINATIONS*

*Cloud capped peaks fill the eyes
In the Spring sunshine.
Their names are written in beautiful characters
And posted in order of merit.
How I hate this silk dress
That conceals a poet.
I lift my head and read their names
In powerless envy."[1]*

Yu Xuanii   c. 860 A.D.

The poem above illustrates one of the restrictions placed upon women by the Confucian system of government: women were not eligible to take the imperial scholarly examinations.[2] Since the men who did well on these examinations became the court officials and governors, such exclusion kept women -- except for empresses -- out of official power. Also, since the image of the educated person was the ideal in Chinese society, it also meant that women were cut out of the most prestigious role in China.

Yet, ironically enough, the stress on education was so much a part of Chinese culture that it spilled over into women's roles also. Most women throughout Chinese history could not read or write, but as early as the Han Dynasty (c. 100 B.C.) there was always an elite group of highly educated women. These women generally fell into four major categories:

1) Members of the imperial court -- empresses and concubines
2) Women of the middle or "gentry" class
3) Courtesans
4) Nuns of the Buddhist or Daoist sects

1. Kenneth Rexroth and Ling Zhong, tr. 7 ed., *The Orchid Boat: Women Poets of China* (New York: The Seabury Press, 1972), p. 19.
2. The Empress Wu had tried to include women in the imperial examinations, but the reform ended after her reign.

34

The women of each of these groups knew how to read and write. But what they did with this knowledge and how public they might be with it, might be quite different.

Women of the Imperial Court

Especially during the Han Dynasty there seems to have been a strong tradition of highly educated women. We know particularly three women, all of whom were influenced by each other and who respected each other.

One was Ban Qieyou, an imperial concubine noted for her learning, poetry and her loyalty to the empress. This loyalty was shown by refusing to embarrass the empress by refusing to join the emperor when he asked her to appear in public instead of the empress. She also joined the empress when the emperor exiled her for a time. The poem Ban Qieyou wrote about their exile and the loss of the emperor's love, "The Autumn Fan," became known as a classic poem of China:

"I took a piece of the fine cloth of Qi,
White silk glowing and pure like frosted snow,
And made you a doubled fan of union and joy,
As flawlessly round as the bright moon.
It comes and goes in my Lord's sleeves.
You can wave it and start a cooling breeze.
But I am always afraid that when Autumn comes,
And the cold blasts drive away the heat,
You will store it away in a bamboo case,
And your love of it will stop midway."[3]

Ban Qieyou's niece, Ban Zhao, became even more famous. Like her aunt, Ban Zhao was very well-educated and part of a remarkable family. One brother was a famous Han general who fought on the frontiers of China; the other brother was a famous historian. Ban Zhao married, but her husband died at a young age and she went back to live with her historian brother. This was a rather unusual arrangement -- usually the widow stayed with her husband's family -- but Ban Zhao was such a fine scholar that her brother needed her assistance. After her brother's death the emperor made her the historian of the court and asked her to finish her brother's history of the Han Dynasty.

Besides accomplishing this task, she also wrote documents relating to her other brother's life, poems of her own and a famous book, *Lessons for Women*. These lessons, along with some other writings, became the basis of what young women were taught. As Ban Zhao and her family were Confucian in belief, the major message of the book is that women should be submissive. Here are some of the "lessons" she urged women to follow:[4]

HUMILITY:
"Let a woman modestly yield to others; let her respect others; let her put others first, herself last. Should she do something good, let her not mention it; should she do something

3. Rexroth, p. 3. "Autumn Fan" became the symbol in China for the discarded wife.
4. Nancy Lee Swann, *Ban Zhao: Foremost Scholar of China* (New York: Century Co., 1932), pp. 82-90.

bad, let her not deny it. Let her bear disgrace; let her even endure when others speak or do evil to her. Always let her seem to tremble and to fear....

"Let a woman retire late to bed, but rise early to duties; let her not dread tasks by day or by night. Let her not refuse to perform domestic duties whether easy or difficult.

RESPECT AND CAUTION:
"If husband and wife have the habit of staying together, never leaving one another, and following each other around within the limited space of their own rooms, then they will lust after and take liberties with one another. From such action improper language will arise between the two. This kind of discussion may lead to licentiousness. Out of licentiousness will be born a heart of disrespect to the husband. Such a result comes from not knowing that one should stay in one's proper place.

BE "WOMANLY":
"To guard carefully her chastity; to control her behavior; in every motion to exhibit modesty; and to model each act in the best usage, this is womanly virtue.

"To choose her words with care; to avoid vulgar language; to speak at appropriate times; and not to weary others (with much conversation), may be called the characteristics of womanly words.

"To wash and scrub filth away; to keep clothes and ornaments fresh and clean; to wash the head and bathe the body regularly, and to keep the person free from disgraceful filth, may be called the characteristics of womanly bearing.

"With whole-hearted devotion to sew and to weave; to love not gossip and silly laughter; in cleanliness and order (to prepare) the wine and food for serving guests, may be called the characteristics of womanly work.

WIDOWS:
"Now in the 'Rites' is written the principle that a husband may marry again, but there is no [law] that authorizes a woman to be married the second time.

OBEDIENCE:
"Whenever the mother-in-law says, 'Do not do that,' and if what she says is right, unquestionably the daughter-in-law obeys. Whenever the mother-in-law says, 'Do that,' even if what she says is wrong, still the daughter-in-law submits unfailingly to the command."

Perhaps one of the reasons Ban Zhao's book was preserved by later Confucian scholars was that her advice to women did not conflict with their ideals. Evidently, there were some criticisms of her writings at the time, but they have been lost in history.

Even though Ban Zhao's writing seems to limit women's actions, she did stress the point that girls should receive an education as well as boys:

"Yet only to teach men and not to teach women -- is that not ignoring the essential relation between them? According to the 'Rites,' it is the rule to begin to teach children to read at the age of eight years, and by the age of fifteen years they ought then to be ready for cultural training. Only why should it not be (that girls' education as well as boys' be) according to this principle?"[5]

This stress on girls' education was one that Ban Zhao's pupil learned well. Ban Zhao tutored the woman who later became Empress Deng. The Empress Dowager Deng (see previous chapter) not only was an excellent ruler of China, but she also had court schools for both girls and boys.

5. *Ibid.*, p. 84.

Not all the empresses and women associated with the court of China were so skilled as these three women. But they left a tradition of court ladies being poets or artists that lasted down through the Manchus. The last major empress dowager, for example, proudly pointed to her own scrolls with her poems and calligraphy.

"Gentry" Women

In Imperial China it is this group of educated women that is perhaps least known. They were the ones generally educated just enough to read Ban Zhao's *Lessons for Women* and some of the other books praising submissive wives and daughters-in-law. They occasionally wrote poems or essays, but these might only be circulated within the family. "Respectable" women did not have their writings known to the public. Though we know the names of some women said to be poets, their work was destroyed by their families.[6]

The poetry of one woman from this class of "gentry" is well-known, however. Li Qingzhao (1084-1141 A.D.) is generally considered the best woman poet in Chinese history.

But perhaps the reason her poetry survived the centuries is not only because she was good, but also because of her family. Both her mother and father were well-educated and she married an educated man. She and her husband, Zhao Mingcheng, both wrote poems and even had contests to see who could write the most fitting poem for various occasions. Though he was somewhat dismayed when her poems were better than his, he seems to have been genuinely proud of her. It was partly through his efforts that her poems became well known.

6. Rexroth and Ling, p. 139.
7. Poems and biographical information from Gaiyou Xu, "The Poems of Li Qingzhao," *Publications of the Modern Language Association of America*, Vol. 77, No. 5 (1962), pp. 521–528.

Three of her poems may suggest their life together. The first describes something of the happiness of their days:

"Often remembered are the evenings on the creek
  When wine flowed in the arbor and we lost our way.
It was late, our boat returned after a happy day
  Entering, by mistake, the thicket of lotus clusters.
    As we hurried to get through
      Hurried to get through,
A flock of herons, startled, rose to the sky."[7]

But the two of them were often separated when Zhao Mingcheng had to travel as a government official. Her poem to him suggests her loneliness:

"The scent of red lotus fades, and the mat feels cool.
I loosen my robe
  To board the boat alone.
Who sends a message through the cloud?
  As the swans return in formation
  Moonlight floods the western chamber.
The petals shall fall and water shall flow.
  One kind of longing,
  Two victims of unnamed grief.
There is no way of getting rid of this thought;
  Just as it recedes from the eyebrows,
  In the heart, it swells."

Later, not only did the Tartars invade and destroy their home, but her husband died. Li Qingzhao's later poems tell of her despair:

"The wind pauses, the scent clings to the dust, but
flowers are no more.
It's getting late and yet I am too weary to comb my
hair.
Things are still the same, but he is gone, it is all over;
Tears well up before any word could be said.
They say that Spring is still young at the Shuang
Creek.
I thought of going to take a small boat there.
Only I fear the tiny boats of the Shuang Creek
Can not carry this much care."

Li Qingzhao is probably the best of Chinese women poets, but there were many others. However, most of the well known ones were not from this Chinese "gentry" class.

Courtesans

Another group of educated women were the courtesans. It is rather difficult to define the role of courtesan in Chinese society. Sometimes the courtesan was merely an expensive prostitute. But sometimes she held an almost semi-official role acting as a hostess for governors assigned to different districts. In this capacity she might, like the Tang poet Hung Du, organize banquets, invite poets in for contests, and help carry on political discussions.[8] These women, because they did not have to follow the usual female modesty roles of Confucian society, could have their poems and writings known publicly. A courtesan poet, Guan Panban (8-9th century) was known, for example, not only for the excellence of her poetry, but also for the "Swallow Mansion," an elaborate palace her patron built for her. But this life often depended on the whim of the male and there was always the fear of abandonment and poverty. The following poem suggests a contrast between the elegance of life if the rich men liked a woman and the life of toil for an impoverished woman:

"WRITTEN AT A PARTY
WHERE MY LORD GAVE AWAY
A THOUSAND BOLTS OF SILK

A bolt of silk for each clear toned song.
Still these beauties do not think it is enough.
Little do they know of a weaving girl,
Sitting cold by her window,
Endlessly throwing her shuttle to and fro."[9]

Qian Tao
(11th century)

8. Genevieve Wimsatt, *A Well of Fragrant Waters* (Boston: John W. Luce, 1945), p. 47.
9. Rexroth and Ling, p. 34.

Nuns

More secure in some ways than courtesans in their lives were nuns. Both Buddhist and Daoist Nuns were generally educated and Daoist nuns particularly seem to have made their poetry public. The most famous Daoist nun was You Xuanji. This woman led quite a life. She became known as a poet, fell in love with a married man; though something of an alcoholic she became a nun. She eventually wound up being executed for the murder of her maid.[10] The poem about the examination hall which begins this section is one of hers and perhaps helps to explain the resentment she seemed to feel in her life. As an unmarried woman she had few places to go in society except the nunnery. Yet, being a nun, while still seeing her friends, seems to have had its good moments too as this poem suggests:

"LIVING IN THE SUMMER MOUNTAINS

I have moved to this home of immortals [the nunnery].
Wild shrubs bloom everywhere.
In the front garden, trees
Spread their branches for clothes racks.
I sit on a mat and float wine cups
In the cool spring.
Beyond the window railing
A hidden path leads away
Into the dense bamboo grove.
In a gauze dress
I read among my disordered
Piles of books.
I take a leisurely ride
In the painted boat,
And chant poems to the moon.
I drift at ease, for I know
The soft wind will blow me home."[11]

These women, the educated women of China, did have much to offer to the culture of China, particularly in the field of poetry. But they were an exceptional group who received an education largely because of their economic background or their special roles in society. It would not be until much later in Chinese history that reformers would begin to work for changes that would consider all Chinese women as eligible for education.

Points To Consider

1. In what ways did their families aid some of the better known educated women of imperial China?

2. Some articles about Ban Zhao describe her as the first "feminist" writer. More recent historians have seen her as something of a traitor to her sex. What evidence from her writings and life would support the first judgment? What evidence would support the second view?

3. Why were the courtesan women more likely to have their poems known than women of the "gentry"?

10. Biographical information from Genevieve Wimsatt, *Selling Wilted Peonies* (New York: Columbia University Press, 1936). Readers might also be interested in a modern mystery novel, *The Willow Pattern*, written about her by Robert vanGulik. As he re-creates her story, she was innocent of the murder.

11. Rexroth and Ling, p. 18.

Women and Education in China: An Activity To Interpret Sources

The educated woman was both admired and looked upon with suspicion in different eras of Chinese history. The following quotations suggest different attitudes toward women's education. Some of the sources are summaries of historical trends; other quotations reflect individual experience. In this activity, try to determine whether it is a *primary* or *secondary* source describing Chinese women. Work in small groups or as individuals. Record your answers on a sheet of paper. Before you begin to decide how to classify each source, discuss the terms "primary" and "secondary" sources within your group.

Primary Sources:

Eye witness accounts of people who actually were involved in or saw the events described in writing or pictures. Primary sources have the advantage of the observer having immediate contact with the event. However, their reporting may be distorted by limitations of their points of view.

Secondary Sources:

Interpretations of events by people who did not witness them. They may be by scholars -- such as historians -- who collect a great deal of source material about an event.

Evaluate each of the following eight sources as follows:

Check one

_____ Primary Source
_____ Secondary Source
_____ Not Sure

Write a short explanation of why you selected "primary," "secondary" or "not sure" for each source.

1. The following is from the biography of Ban Zhao by Fan Veh, written in the fifth century A.D.
"Ban Zhao also wrote 'Lessons for Women' in seven chapters, (a treatment which) affords assistance in the education of women... Ma Rung was so pleased with the treatise that he ordered the wives and daughters (of his family) to practice its precepts. Ban Zhao's younger sister-in-law, Ts'ao Feng-sheng, likewise talented and cultured, wrote essays which are worth reading, in which she took issue with Ban Zhao." Translated and quoted in Nancy Lee Swann, *Ban Zhao: Foremost Woman Scholar of China*, (N.Y.: Century, 1932), p. 41.

2. **"The woman with no talent is the one who has merit."** Quotation attributed to Confucius, quoted in Dennis Bloodworth, *The Chinese Looking Glass*, (N.Y.: Farrar, Straus & Co., 1967), p. 73.

3. A conversation between a Chinese mother and daughter in 1900 written in the daughter's autobiography:
"Training girls is my business. You will start embroidering next year. Your feet are still too big, and I haven't finished with them yet. If you are like this when you marry, people will say that your mother did not bring you up properly."

"But I want to study," I said, *"Am I not a human being like my brothers?"*

"What a joke! Like your brothers! They study to become officials and earn money, but you are a girl. You can only be a good wife and good mother, and learn to serve your parents-in-law well and run a home. What is the use of your studying?" Source: Xie Bingying: *Girl Rebel*, (N.Y.: John Day, 1940), p. 24.

4. A Chinese woman described her medical school classes in Japan:
"The professor read his notes aloud, page by page, in class, and all the students scribbled at top speed without once looking up. It was important to get every thing down, as many students could not afford to buy books, and the library facilities were not such as would enable the

students to do regular assigned readings." Source: *Buwei Yang Chao: Autobiography of a Chinese Woman*, (N.Y.: John Day, 1943), pp. 140-41.

5. "*It is refreshing to find records of educated Chinese women even though these records, extending over thousands of years, show a very small proportion of intellectual women. It is evident, too, that the proportion varied at different times and in different parts of China, leaving some periods and some places dark indeed.*" Source: Mary Raleigh Anderson, *A Cycle in the Celestial Kingdom*, (Mobile: Heiter-Stake, 1943), p. 26.

6. Qiu Jin, the Chinese revolutionary wrote:
"*Ah, slowly, slowly a thread of light is piercing the black darkness of our woman's realm which shut in on all sides, for four times one thousand years has existed until the present day. Ah! endless, endless, the long road, how shall we compass it? One hears of those who find the first impulse easy; those who find complete fulfillment hard.... The mirror of better days is not far distant; looking back, the past ten years, condition of students' realm in this our Central State can be realized: In schools, to be established, we should hold examinations to bring prosperity in our time, our generation. Chanting aloud the Classics, heads held high in air, must resolutely be discarded. As grain slowly expands, so must we slowly practice foreign words, phrases, essays, literature. Who does not say: modern youth, modern youth, their ideals are great, but the bright sun of their understanding is obscured; their true principles are not yet evident.*" Quoted in Florence Ayscough, *Chinese Women: Yesterday and Today* (Boston: Houghton Mifflin, 1937), p. 163.

7. "*Girls were almost exclusively trained for their duties in the domestic sphere. The chief aim in a girl's education was the inculcation of ancient stereotypes of female conduct. All the older members of the family assisted in informing what she may, or may not do, in all sorts of situations, particularly in relation to her brothers, father, mother, uncles, and her future husband and his parents.*" Source: Elisabeth Croll, *Feminism and Socialism in China* (London: Routledge and Kegan Paul, 1978).

8. Luhchan, a nineteenth century Chinese author, wrote a book *Female Instructor* in which he is quoted as saying:
"*Rearing the silkworm and working cloth are the most important of the employments of a female; preparing and serving up the food for her household and setting in order the sacrifices, follow next, each of which must be attended to. After them study and learning can fill up the time.*" Source: Quoted in Margaret Burton, *The Education of Women in China* (New York: Fleming Revell, 1911), p. 13.

D. Women and Religion

It is difficult to make generalizations about Chinese religious views; and it is just as difficult to make generalizations about what Chinese women did with their religion. Many Chinese took parts of various religions, Buddhism, Daoism, Confucianism, Shammanism and later Christianity, to form their own faiths. Though most might agree on ancestor-worship, their lives here on earth might be shaped by several beliefs. The role of women in these beliefs has not been adequately researched, but there are some observations that might be made.

While Confucianism offered support to the mother of sons by stressing the respect she should receive, it did not necessarily offer the childless woman or the neglected wife much consolation. Other religions like Buddhism, and later Christianity, offered more personal intervention in human's lives. In times of illness a mother might pray for Buddha's intercession to save her child. The mother might even promise the child to the temple if he or she got well.

The Buddhist religion also offered an alternative to marriage; women could become nuns. Sometimes they did so because, as widows or rejected concubines, they had nowhere else to go. For example, the Empress Wu, before coming to the court for a second time, stayed in a Buddhist nunnery. But other women devoted their lives to prayer and keeping up the nunneries which were often a refuge for travelers. One British traveler described the Buddhist nuns she saw in the 1880's:

"Among the villages, one not infrequently sees a woman in a gray cotton tunic and conical splint hat, with a shaven head and natural feet, and carrying a bag and basket on her arm. Her attire distinguishes her from other Chinese women. The long gray gown and shaven head are the badges of her religious order, that of a Buddhist nun. The bag holds the rice, and the basket the fruit and vegetables, given her at the doors of the houses before which she halts....

"In the gleanings of her morning walk, the nun has enough for herself, and for some other nuns too young or too old to go out and gather for themselves. Her home is a temple, sometimes extensive in its grounds, fine in its architecture.... It has a main building, in which are immense figures of Buddha, and lesser halls with images of the saints. Before these the nuns chant liturgies three times a day.... Around the chief temple are courts with small apartments where the nuns sleep and work. These women are the only inmates of the place. They sew and spin, and bring up children to be nuns like themselves.... [These children] are sold to the nunnery when two or three years old, for three or four dollars apiece; and the nuns, each buying as many as she can support, bring them up. Sometimes a nun thus has as many as twenty little girls under her immediate care, and subject to no authority but hers.... [The nuns] buy those that are past the first diseases of infancy, and healthy and attractive. As soon as the girls are

Chinese Buddhist Nuns, c. 1900.

old enough, they are taught to weave and embroider and read. A good teacher is employed to instruct them, and they often become fine scholars.

"At fifteen, the little girl ceases to eat animal food, has her head clean-shaven, and puts on the dress of a nun. It is said that no coercion is used in keeping girls in the nunnery, but that none of them ever choose to leave it and return to their parents. They are much more comfortable in the nunnery than they could be with the poverty-stricken parents who sold them.

"The nuns frequently make long excursions in their own boats, bringing home boat-loads of fruits or vegetables. They weave with skill, and embroider exquisitely, and are almost the only women who know how to read. They are called to chant at death-beds, to dispel the evil influences in streets and houses, and receive pay for special petitions to their gods. Their incomes are large and their lives easy. Taken together, they appear strong, portly, and comfortable beyond other Chinese women..."[1]

1. Adele Fielde, *Pagoda Shadows* (Boston: A. G. Corthell, 1884), pp. 108–112.

Perhaps most central to Buddhist women in China was the worship of the female god of mercy, Guan Yin. . Her place in the Chinese religion was rather like that of the Virgin Mary in the Catholic religion. She was said to help those who were in trouble, particularly those who were shipwrecked or spiritually lost. This female god seems to have started out male, at least Indian Buddhism at first represented a male Lord of Mercy. But by the twelfth century A.D., Guan Yin became to be represented as a woman.[2] Her representations have changed in various ways throughout Chinese history. There are many stories and legends about her and her respect in Chinese buddhism was second only to Buddha, himself.

One woman described how she felt as a child watching her mother pray to the household shrine of Guan Yin:

"...I liked best to tiptoe in when the red candles were burning before the lovely bronze statuette of the gracious and beautiful Guan Yin, the Buddhist Goddess of Mercy, and the fragrant smoke of incense ascended in slow spirals while my mother, with hands palm to palm, would first bow low with her forehead to the floor, and then look up, with a rapt expression, as she made her petition to the goddess or repeated her devotions. Sometimes she would ask me to kneel beside her and take part. I did not like to do this although I cannot say why, and I used to wonder why she spent so much time talking to a bronze image on a shelf. I liked to watch and listen although I did not know what she was saying. I never learned.

"Each of the ladies in our household had a Guan Yin in her room. She was the patron goddess of our woman's world. But that of my mother was the most beautiful. Before it were two brass candlesticks, two vases of flowers, and an incense burner. In front of these were five

dishes of wax fruit: tangerines, pears, apples, peaches...."[3]

Daoism was similar to Buddhism in its treatment of women. Daoist women could also become nuns although they did not shave their heads as Buddhist nuns did. Women could also play a major part in the religion. One of the "Eight Immortals," He Xiangu, of Daoism was thought to be female. Further, there seems in Daoism a belief in male and female principles as underlying the universe, joined as a symbol in the phoenix or in Yin-Yang.[4] As the Daoist religion developed, a female god was added to their pantheon of gods. The god was the Jade Lady whose shrines seem to have been important in South China, particularly.[5]

Some of the ceremonies connected with Daoism included both men and women sharing religious tasks. Whether or not this mixture of women and men in public was in itself shocking -- or whether the rumors were true -- Daoists were sometimes accused of carrying on "immoral orgies." Priests and nuns, however, did not have to take vows of poverty, chastity or obedience and friends might visit them.[6] Daoist nuns were, thus, sometimes accused of improper behavior. One of the most famous Daoist nuns, for example, was the poet You Xuanji whose active social life was not much changed by her entry into the nunnery.

Besides Buddhism and Daoism there were beliefs in various folk gods and ghosts. Female figures, like water

2. Juliet Bredon and Igor Mitrophanow, *The Moon Year* (Shanghai: Kelly & Walsh, 1927), p. 184.
3. Suling Wong (Earl Herbert Cressy), *Daughter of Confucius* (New York: Farrar, Straus & Giroux, Inc., 1952), pp. 28–30.
4. Kenneth Scott Latourette, *The Chinese: Their History and Culture* (New York: Macmillan, 1971), p. 553.
5. Bredon, pp. 282–283.
6. Eloise Hibbert, *Embroidered Gauze* (London: John Lane, 1938), p. 211.

fairies, dragon ladies and fox women, often played roles in these beliefs, sometimes acting for the good, sometimes not. A typical tale from the Tang Dynasty period is:

"Southeast of the walled city of Khotan there is a great river which irrigates the fields of the entire nation. Suddenly its flow was interrupted. The king of that nation inquired about it of the monk Luohong, who said that it was the work of a dragon. The king then made offering to the dragon. From the midst of the water came a woman, skimming the waves. She saluted and said, 'Your hand-maiden's husband is dead. It is her wish to obtain a great vassal [nobleman] as a husband. Then the water will be once more as of old.' One of the great vassals [noblemen] begged leave to go, and the whole nation went to see him off. That vassal went into the water with carriage, rig, and white horse, but did not drown. After he had reached the middle of the river, the white horse floated out with a sandalwood drum and a manuscript in an envelope on its back. They took out the manuscript, which said, 'Let the great drum be hung southeast of the city wall-- should marauders come it will sound of itself.' Afterwards, whenever raiders came, the drum did sound of itself."[7]

In the 16th century, Christian missionaries began to arrive in China. Christianity seems to have had special appeal for women. Like Buddhism there was in Christianity a central female figure, the Virgin Mary, of mercy and intercession. Also, Western missionaries sometimes brought with them a sense of more equal roles for women. With the Catholic nuns and the Protestant "Bible women," single women had positions of participation in the religion and in education.

Until the Communists came to power in 1949, there were followers of various religions in China. However, the most important god for women -- whether or not they identified themselves as Buddhist -- seems to have been the female god, Guan Yin.

Points To Consider

1. What specific things about Buddhism might have had special appeal to Chinese women?

2. In what ways did Daoism offer similar comforts for women?

2. On the following page are pictures of various statues and paintings of the female god of mercy, Guan Yin, arranged chronologically from c. 900 A.D. to c. 1700 A.D.

   A. List things that you notice about each picture, 1-4.

   B. In what specific ways does the god stay the same in each of these time periods?

   C. In what ways does she change?

   D. Which ones show her as the most powerful? As most beautiful? What things might this indicate about women in China in each time period?

7. As quoted in Edward Schafer, *The Divine Woman* (Berkeley: University of California Press, 1973), p. 120.

Guan Yin c. 900

Guan Yin c. 1056

Guan Yin c. 1300

Guan Yin c. 1700

E. Women Warriors

Chinese history contains countless stories of women being involved in war. These stories, told through the generations, often became an inspiration for Chinese women in this century when facing civil war or fighting against the Japanese.[1] Considering the length of Chinese history, it is not surprising that women might have played various roles, but this role of woman warrior seems especially to contrast with traditional Chinese culture.

First of all, the Confucian ideal was of the secluded woman, submissive to the males in her family and her life confined to domestic activities. Second, the military itself was not seen as admirable in Chinese culture. The scholar was the ideal; the soldier was seen as merely necessary. For example, Song Meiling's family did not wish her to marry General Chiang Kai-Shek even though he might control China; military men were not quite respectable.

Yet, the woman warrior seems to appear throughout Chinese history. Some historians have suggested that the very harshness of women's lives in China made them stern and brave enough to face the hardships of war. Also, the tales of the "ideal" women of China frequently included the self-sacrifice and bravery of women in protecting the lives of husbands or parents. Certain peoples of China -- the Mongol, Khitan or the Hakka -- had traditions of women being involved in military actions. One Liao empress, for example, personally led her troops in battle against the Song in 1005 A.D. and beat them.[2]

There were so many women warriors in Chinese history that an encyclopedia published by the Chinese in 1726 had five volumes concerning the lives of women generals and military leaders.[3] The most famous of the women warriors --- the Joan of Arc of China -- was Hua Mulan. Not much actually is known of her life but she seems to have lived in the 5th century A.D. According to the poems and plays written about her, Mulan's father was told to join the army. But since he was ill, she went in his place. She fought and led troops for twelve years before victory brought her home.[4] Other women warriors from imperial China included the widow of Feng Bao, who as a grandmother fought as a soldier, and Qin Liang You, a woman the Ming emperor made commander-in-chief of all his armies after she had put down various rebellions.[5]

Besides fighting as individuals, women also fought together in units in later Chinese history. For example, in the White Lotus Rebellion (1796-1804) units of women fought with the

1. A book recently published by a Chinese American author suggests that the example of these women is still culturally important. See Maxine Hong Kingston, *The Woman Warrior: Memoirs of a Girlhood Among Ghosts* (New York: Vintage Books, 1977).
2. Karl Wittfogel and Feng Jiasheng, *History of Chinese Society* (Philadelphia: American Philosophical Society, 1949), p. 200.
3. Ida Belle Lewis, *The Education of Girls in China* (New York: Columbia University Press, 1919), pp. 15–16.
4. Florence Ayscough, *Chinese Women Yesterday and Today* (Boston: Houghton Mifflin Co., 1937), pp. 216–222.
5. L. C. Arlington, "China's Heroes of the Past," *Tian Xia Monthly*, Vol. V, No. 5 (December, 1937), p. 476.

men and a woman named Wang was one of the commanders.[6]

In the Taiping Rebellion (1850-1864), women fought in separate units, but they were a major part of the uprising. Many of the women in the uprising were Hakka who did not bind their feet and therefore could fight well. There are many descriptions of the Taiping women; the following suggests the skill and bravery for which they were praised:

"In the Taiping army there was a woman by the name of Xiao Sanniang, known as the 'woman commander'.... She was at least twenty, tall and long-armed, a great general on horseback. She could shoot an arrow with either hand. When the Taiping army captured Zhenjiang, she led several hundred women soldiers and climbed the city wall, braver and fiercer than the men. All who met them fell back...."[7]

A third rebellion in which women took part was the Boxer Uprising (1900 A.D.). The Boxers seem to have been part of secret societies like the Triad and White Lotus who had opposed the Manchus. These groups included women, particularly in the Boxer's case in associated societies. The Red Lantern sect of the Boxers was made up primarily of young women; the daughter of boat people, Hunaglian Shengmu, became the leader. These women carried red handkerchiefs and lanterns and supposedly had supernatural powers to stop foreign bullets.[8] Like the Boxers they were defeated when lead proved more powerful than magic.

6. Victor Purcell, *The Boxer Uprising* (Cambridge: Cambridge University Press, 1963), pp. 155–156.
7. As quoted in Vincent Y. C. Shih, *The Taiping Ideology* (Seattle: University of Washington, 1967), p. 62.
8. Victor Purcell, *The Boxer Uprising*, pp. 235–239.

Mulan returning from war.

In the twentieth century, the tradition of women warriors continued. In the Chinese Revolution, "Dare To Die" units were formed of Chinese women. One of these women, Xie Bingying, described how she was received when she came into a village on horseback:

"I arrived at Jiayou first and alone. In order to look for living quarters, I had to ride about the streets, back and forth. 'Ah, here comes a girl soldier!' 'The girl soldiers have arrived!' 'A girl officer on horseback!' Such cries turned whole crowds of women folk out to see me. As I was surrounded by the crowd, I could only whip the horse and hurry on. I was truly afraid of a fall, as I had never ridden before in my life. You can imagine the embarrassment I was in.... Some addressed me as 'old general,' some as 'lady teacher,' some as 'lady officer,' and one boy called me 'lady generalissimo.' I was sweating all over and my face was burning hot, and I did not know what to do. I realized that I had become an old curiosity-- or rather a new monstrosity. Both men and women stared at me from head to foot, and I believe they even counted the numbers of my hair. An old woman said: 'I have lived eighty years without seeing a short-haired, big-footed, uniformed female devil like you. Ha! ha!' We all joined in her laughter.

"Another woman of over forty came and offered me tea, for which I was truly thankful. Besides, she said something which was painful-- yet really not painful-- to me. She said, 'If such a blithe young girl should die on the battlefield, what will her parents feel at home?' I said calmly, 'Madam, I am ready to die for the revolution and the people. As for the parents, of course we are sorry to leave them, but....."[9]

This regiment of women was later disbanded when Chiang Kai-Shek took power.

While Guomindang women generally did not fight with the army in the Chinese Civil War of the 1930's and 1940's, Communist women did. How many Communist women were actually involved in the fighting -- not acting as nurses or support forces -- is somewhat unclear. There seems to have been at least one segregated regiment of about eight hundred women soldiers.

Two Chinese Communist women seem to have been in command of regular Red troops, He Ying and Kang Kejing. The former was killed in the fighting, but Kang Kejing later married the best of the Red generals, Zhu De. Though she spent most of her time acting as a medic or as propagandist, she did see some fighting.

Kang Kejing described to an American reporter one combat experience in which she was the only woman who participated in the fighting. For awhile she was even elected commander by the male soldiers. Later she was told that the enemy especially feared this girl commander.[10]

The ideal of the "woman warrior" or "girl commander" is one that has been present in Chinese society but primarily as an exceptional ideal. Chinese women now are part of the People's Liberation Army and there is a squadron of Chinese women pilots. However, the women seem to be largely in military support roles. It appears that women pilots are trained for transport planes rather than fighter planes. For example, an article published in China on these women fliers describes the airlifting of sandbags to flood victims.[11] In the 1940's, Red Army commanders were

9. Xi Bingying, Adet and Anor Lin, tr, *Girl Rebel: The Autobiography of Xie Bingying* (New York: John Day Co., reprinted Harper, Row Pub., 1940), pp. 91-92.
10. Helen Foster Snow, *The Chinese Communists* (Westport, Ct.: Greenwood Publishing, 1977), pp. 216-217.
11. *New Women in New China*, (Peking: Foreign Language Press).

Women pilots of the Chinese People's Liberation Army.

Xie Bingying

trained at high level military schools which are not open to women.[12] There is little evidence that this policy has changed or that women are not still excluded from high ranking military positions in the Chinese Red Army.

Points To Consider

1. What things in Chinese traditional culture might have acted against a woman being in the military? What things might have acted for a woman warrior?

2. Why might so many women of China, even though not soldiers themselves, tell stories of Mulan and identify with her?

3. According to Marxist ideas, Communists were supposed to bring more equality to the women of China. What would you say might be the attitude of the Communists toward women in the military?

12. Jane Price, "Women and Leadership in the Chinese Communist Movement, 1921–1945," *Bulletin of Concerned Asian Scholars,* Vol. 7, No. 1, (January-March, 1975), pp. 19–22.

Chapter 3

Women in Traditional China

Chapter Contents

A. Stages of Women's Lives: Introduction

The previous selections dealt with women in historical China in rather exceptional roles. Part III is concerned with "traditional" Chinese women -- in other words with the common roles for women from about the Sung Dynasty (c. 900 A.D.) to relatively modern times.

The following information is taken from a study of the village of Gaixiangong in east-central China. This study was conducted by an anthropologist in the 1930's right before China became involved in World War II. Some changes were occurring in Gaixiangong at that time because of new laws, factory jobs becoming available and increasing contacts with people outside the village. However, the village people were still usually "traditional" in their outlook and customs. Therefore, although this data is from one small Chinese village in the 1930's, it can be considered to be representative of customs and outlook of peasants in much of traditional China.

Data on the Village of Gaixiangong:[1]

Marriage Customs

1. All adults were expected to marry. Every man must have a son to perform funeral rites for him and his wife. It is considered an obligation of parents to find wives for their sons.

2. Persons were not to marry someone with the same surname (family name).

3. Many villages in traditional China were made up of all one surname.

4. Customary -- and most approved -- marriages were arranged with a man or woman outside of the village.

5. A girl usually left her village to live with her husband's family.

6. Sometimes, where there was a daughter but no son, a marriage was arranged with the daughter and a man who was willing to take the family surname and live in the woman's home. A man who agreed to such a "uxorilocal" marriage was often looked down on for contracting such a marriage.

7. Although the girl's family received a bride price from the groom's family at the time of the marriage, they were expected to provide her with household goods to set her up in her new home.

8. Generally, women in north China only worked in the fields in times of great hardship. Traditionally, women in this village had raised silk worms at home. This had been an

1. Information from: Xiaotong Fei, *Peasant Life in China* (London: Routledge & Kegan Paul, 1962), p. 38.

important source of family income. However, beginning in the 1920's, factories were replacing home production of silk in this area of China.

9. Sometimes a poor peasant family would adopt a girl when she was about five years old as a future wife for their son. She lived with her adopted family and worked for them. When old enough, she married the son of her adopted family.

Roles of Daughters and Sons

1. The son was responsible for ancestor worship and carried on the family name.

2. At an early age, children contributed to the family economy. Girls were considered especially useful to watch younger children, they helped their mothers in household chores and, in this particular village, they worked in the home silk industry.

3. The sons inherited the family property. Women could not inherit even if there were no sons.

4. Sons were obligated to take care of their parents in their old age. The married daughters

might send gifts to elderly parents but were not obligated to support them.

5. A married daughter will not offer sacrifices to ancestors of her own parents' family. After her own death she receives sacrifices from her husband's family -- not from her own -- if she has given birth to a live son.

Village Statistics

1. The total area of cultivated village land is 3,065 mou. If this area were equally allotted to 360 households, it would mean that each household could only occupy a piece of land about 8.5 mou (or 1.2 acres) in size. Each mou of land can produce in a normal year six bushels of rice. About twenty-seven bushels of rice is needed for the consumption of one man, one woman, and one child. In other words, to obtain sufficient food a family group of three needs a piece of land of about five mow. The present size of land holdings is hardly sufficient to provide an average household with a normal livelihood.

2. 1935 Census:[2]

Age	Male	Female	Total
71+	4	15	19
66–70	10	19	29
61–65	14	32	46
56– 0	30	39	69
51–55	40	38	78
46–50	26	29	55
41–45	45	38	83
36–40	69	55	124
31–35	64	45	109
26–30	75	61	136
21–25	63	52	115
16–20	68	54	122
11–15	72	61	133
6–10	73	59	132
–5	118	87	205
	––	––	3
Total	771	684	1458

Points To Consider

1. List specific reasons why parents might want to:

   A. have a boy baby
   B. have a girl baby
   C. limit the size of their family

2. According to the 1935 census, how many girls were there in Gaixiangong between birth to ten? List reasons that could account for these differences. What do you feel is the most likely reason or reasons?

3. In what age group do you first have more women than men in Gaixiangong? In what age group do you have more than three times more women than men? How do you account for this?

4. There are five times as many widows (women) as widowers (men) in the United States. Considering that almost everyone married in traditional China, it would seem by the number of old women that a similar imbalance occurred in China. How do you account for this trend under such different circumstances?

2. This was the first census conducted of the village — soon after this World War II prevented additional systematic record keeping.

A. 1. Women in Youth

Infancy:

*"No one is glad when a girl is born;
By her the family sets no store."* [1]
Fu Xuan (278 A.D.)

*"When a son is born, he is laid
down on couches, and is given a
piece of jade to play with. When
a daughter is born, she is laid on
the floor, and is given a tile to
play with."* [2]
*The Book of Odes
c. 800 B.C.*

*"A gifted girl is not as valuable
as a good for nothing boy."*
Chinese proverb

*"Ten daughters do not in any case
equal the value of one son."*
Chinese proverb

*"[Girls are] goods on which one
loses."* [3]
Chinese proverb

Among traditional Chinese peasants
the birth of a girl baby was usually
not a time of joy. As the data in the
introduction indicates, there were
few benefits to a Chinese family in
having a girl:

--- usually she was married in her
late teens

--- upon marriage she moved to
her husband's village and home

--- her husband's family had the
right to her labor and children

--- daughters were not obligated to
take care of elderly parents

--- daughters belonged to their
husband's family so did not
carry on the family name and
were not "links" in the chain of
generations. Sacrificial duties
to dead ancestors were carried
out by sons or the sons' wives.

If a family already had a son, a
daughter might be welcomed as a
future babysitter and household
worker. Some Chinese families
welcomed a first girl child and some
even felt to have on eldest daughter
was the best family situation.
However, if the second or third
children were also girls, the family
was often so distressed that these
girls were given names that
expressed this family displeasure: [4]
   Xia Duo (Little Too-Many)
   Xiao Zhou (Little Unpleasantness)
   Xiao Chui (Little Mistake)

Boys were never named with a
derogatory term. They were often
called:
   Xi (Joy)
   Luo (Happiness)

It was not too surprising that in
traditional China the practice of
controlling population by female
infanticide was considered to be
widespread. Although a Chinese

1. Quoted in Judith Stacey, "When Patriarchy
Kowtows: The Significance of the Chinese Family
Revolution for Feminist Theory," *Feminist Studies,*
Vol. 2, No. 2/3 (1976), p. 65.
2. Quoted in Wong Alene, "Women in China: Past
and Present," in Carolyn Matthiasson (ed.) *Many
Sisters* (New York: The Free Press, 1974), p. 231.
3. Maurice Freedman, *Lineage Organization in
Southeastern China* (London: University of London,
1958), p. 31.
4. Martin C. Yang, *A Chinese Village* (New York:
Columbia University Press, 1945), pp. 124–125.

cultural ideal was to have large families, most peasants could not afford them. As the figures from the village of Gaixiangong in the introduction show, there simply was not enough land available to most peasants to support a large family. Although conditions varied depending on location and individual wealth of peasant families, they usually had to restrict their family size in accordance with their limited land holdings.[5]

Folk methods of contraception were widely used and, although abortions were illegal until recently, there is evidence that they were quite a common form of birth control within traditional Chinese families. However, there often was a desire for male children, but no more female children. In this case the likely method of restricting family size was to kill baby girls at birth or to neglect them through less feeding or care so that only the strongest survived infancy. Natural disasters such as droughts, earthquakes, and famines were common in China's history. Even in good years the poorer peasants were often close to starvation. Family size had to be controlled and girl babies were considered to be the most expendable family members -- to raise a girl was a luxury. There are few statistics or other objective, measurable evidence on infanticide in traditional China. It was not a practice people openly admitted to. However, infanticide was common enough to be commented on frequently in Chinese literature, in travelers' accounts and by missionaries. For example, there were various prohibitions against drowning infants in public wells. Both the Guomindang and Communist governments passed specific laws agains infanticide -- an indication that it was practiced and there was a need to outlaw it.[6] One traveler in the early 1930's came across this sign on a bridge near the city of Fuzhou: "Girls may not be

drowned here."[7]

Babyhood:

If a baby daughter survived the first few weeks of life, many observers have felt that they were treated in much the same way as boy babies, until the age of four or five. By modern western standards, in some ways all babies of Chinese peasants seem to have been neglected. In other ways they may seem "spoiled." Chinese parents often indulged their babies, no matter of what sex.

The following description was written by a Chinese anthropologist. His description is probably typical of childcare in much of traditional China. As you read this excerpt, notice in what specific ways babies of both sexes are treated alike and in what ways differently.

"All infants are fed at the mother's breast as a matter of course. If the unfortunate mother has no milk, porridge or cow's milk will be administered freely. The local people feel that an infant whose mother has no milk has rather poor chances of survival. The breast is given the infant as soon as he/she cries and is taken away when the little one has gone to sleep...

"Handling the diaper is exclusively a women's concern, largely, the mother's. At each change of diaper, the lower part of the infant's body may be rinsed with water. Apart from this, there is no idea of a regular bath. Diapers are changed as soon as the mother can manage it. If the mother is hard pressed by work, the

5. There has been an extensive amount of scholarship which shows that the large joint family was uncommon in traditional China and that the typical Chinese family was in fact rather small. For one summary of this scholarship see: Olga Lang, *Chinese Family and Society* (New Haven, Connecticut: Yale University Press, 1946), Chapter XII: "The Type and Size of the Family."
6. Henry DeL'eew, *Cities of Sin* (New York: Harrison Smith and Robert Haas, 1933), p. 112.
7. Judith Stacey, "Patriarchy," p. 105.

A mother holding her daughter.

infant may stay wet for a couple of hours. But from the time the infant is two or three months old, it is seldom left alone. If the mother is not with it, some other member of the household, a girl, or older woman, and occasionally a man, will be there to hold it, give it food, fondle it, or make it smile. When the mother goes to the market, the infant is often tied securely to her, its stomach against her back. In this manner it may be carried for considerable distances. When the infant is a male, he may be carried in this way until he is two or three years of age. Females are as a rule carried for shorter periods.

"Every infant illness is attributed to evil spirits who may be unfavorably disposed toward past or present members of the family....

"Every cure known and believed in by the people will be resorted to in order to restore a child's health. Of course, the effort expended for a male child is considerably more than that for a female.

"After the death of a child less than one year of age no ceremony takes place. The little body is simply taken out of the house, rolled in a straw mat, and buried in some unused ground outside the town. Wild dogs *will search it out and eat it.[8] Rich families have been known to use coffins for their children who died less than one year after birth. There is no rigid rule on this matter, however, and it seems to be decided by the financial ability of the family."[9]*

Childhood:

At the age of four or five the period of indulging Chinese children as babies ended. Sons went off to work with their fathers and, if they were from gentry families, would no longer sleep in the women's quarters. Daughters lives also changed:

--- They were often put in charge of younger brothers or sisters -- it was common to see a small child with a baby almost as big as herself strapped to her back.

--- They began their training in domestic chores and crafts such as spinning, weaving or raising of silk worms.

--- To a certain extent village girls were segregated, they were at least discouraged from playing with boys outside their immediate families or neighborhoods. Gentry girls were more strictly segregated to the women's quarters and were not even allowed to play with their brothers.

--- Footbinding began.

--- Especially if a family was in difficulties because of extreme poverty, it was usually at this age that girls might be sold. There were at least three motives for buyers acquiring Chinese girls. Either they might buy girl children as future servants, as future daughters-in-law and household helpers or as future prostitutes for brothels.

The following excerpts describe something of these occurrences

common to the childhood of many women in traditional China. The harshness of the lives of many Chinese peasants and the extremely low status of young Chinese women made aspects of traditional girlhood often inhumanly severe. During these years daughters learned tough lessons on survival in a system that continued to discriminate against them until they reached old age.

Childhood: Learning Adult Skills

As this next selection indicates, sometimes learning an adult skill and being considered a valuable part of the adult world was not unpleasant. This description is from an early 20th century autobiography of a Chinese woman. Xie Bingying came from a prosperous, large family and later her older brother made sure that she was allowed an education. However, her mother did not approve of her going to school and insisted that she learn to spin like the other village girls.

"The autumn wind carried with it the fragrance of cassias. The moon was shining in the clear sky, the stars were twinkling near the horizon, and children were racing with their own

8. For example, an expression that relates to older children is: "Good, the child is out of reach of dogs!" quoted in Martin C. Yang, *A Chinese Village* (New York: Columbia University Press, 1945), p. 11. In 1900 an English woman traveler reported the following experience with "baby towers."
"These [bad smells] are wafted from the Baby Towers, two of which we had to pass. They are square in shape, with small windows about twelve feet from the ground, somewhat resembling pigeon-towers. These strange dovecots are built to receive the bodies of such babies as die too young to have fully developed souls, and therefore there is no necessity to waste coffins on them.... Some of these poor little creatures are brought here alive and left to die, and some of these have been rescued and carried to foundling hospitals... Most of the bodies deposited here are those of girl-babies who have been intentionally put to death..." (from C. F. Gordon Cumming, *Wanderings in China,* London: William Blackwood and Sons, 1900), p. 306.
9. Francis L. K. Xu, *Under the Ancestor's Shadow* (Stanford, CA: Standford University Press, 1967), pp. 204-206.

Small sister carrying baby brother.

shadows in the yards or playing hide and seek. But I, a little eight-year-old girl, had already begun a grown-up's work.

"Besides my sister-in-law and myself spinning in the moonlight, there were two distant paternal aunts and a neighbor girl named Zhen.

"Every girl who grew up in our village, when she reached the age of seven or eight, had to be taught to spin cotton and do linen and needle work....

"...Mother said, 'If you can spin fast and if our own cotton isn't enough for you, we can go and buy some at Nandian.'

"'I don't like to spin and weave, I can't use so much cloth,' I said.

"'It is not for you now, but for your trousseau. If you will make up your mind to weave and have twenty trunks of clothing to carry to your future mother-in-law's home, how proud we shall be!' ...

"...I began to be interested in spinning, especially when working in the moonlight; there was really no happier moment! In winter I spun indoors. There were many inconveniences. Mother wanted to save oil and did not light the lamp. It was dark spinning by the light from the fireplace, and my back was cold. In autumn, however, the weather was mild and the moonlight was especially clear. Grandmother would tell us stories, such as 'The Cowherd and the Spinning Maidens' and 'The Lady in the Moon' and 'The Queen of Heaven,' which made the hours at the spinning wheel pleasant. Sometimes when the stories got too interesting everyone would stop the wheels all at once, and ask, 'What's the ending?'

"'The ending was that the lazy little girls stopped their work,' Grandmother would say.

"The swinging rhythm of the spinning wheel in that deep and quiet night was like music from the valleys. The breeze blew softly over our heads, and carried with it the fragrance of flowers that made one feel fascinated by the charm of the night."[10]

Childhood: Segregation

"The wife of a Daoist priest told a foreign lady that in her next existence she hoped to be born a dog, that she might go where she chose!" quoted in Arthur Smith, Village Life in China.

By six or seven, village peasant girls were expected to help at family chores, bind their feet and play close to home. Although they were not strictly separated from their brothers, cousins or neighborhood boys, they were discouraged from wandering very far.

Gentry girls were quite strictly segregated from boys and usually were confined to the women's quarters of their large compound homes. The following is a young woman's description of a few aspects of the segregated women's world she grew up in as a member of the gentry class. She later left seclusion to go to college and live a more open modern life. However, in this excerpt she points up some of the comforts for women of living in seclusion and some of the formal rules for regulating this segregated household.

"We had a happy time in this women's world of my childhood, in our patrician [wealthy] family behind its bamboo curtain....

"Among the peasantry, Chinese women have much more freedom to go in and out. Their life is, in the nature of the case, more open. Their much smaller and simpler dwellings

10. Xie Bingying, Girl Rebel, The Autobiography of Xie Bingying, Adet and Anor Lin, trs. (New York: John Day & Co., Reprinted Harper & Row, 1940), pp. 18-19.

make impossible the degree of seclusion that was maintained in a gentry family like ours.

"This seclusion of the feminine portion of our household gave it a calm and sheltered aspect, and developed a psychology of naturalness and trust. We were always among friends....

"We fitted into a fixed framework of generation and seniority, to which we conformed without question. This really gave an added freedom, for we had no need to assert ourselves or to strive for position or leadership. That was settled in advance.

"We knew no other world than this....

"Our world embodied those elements of strength which have enabled the Confucian system to survive for over twenty centuries. Take the matter of sex, which is always a potential source of complications. Sexual indifference extends only to brothers and sisters, and not to the cousins and slave girls who were nevertheless thrown together in one household, but our somewhat Puritanical way of life was ordered by strict rules which no one thought of disobeying.

"It is a well-known Confucian rule that when men and women have to pass things to each other their fingers must not touch. With us, clothing belonging to the opposite sex could not be hung in the same closet or on the same bamboo pole to dry. We girls were not allowed to sit on a seat that had been recently been vacated by a man.

"The women kept to their own rooms or visited each other in the kitchen or somewhere in the inner courtyards, and even slave girls were not allowed to go outside the gate for shopping or calling on their friends. If one of the ladies wished to visit a friend or relative, she had first to get permission from grandmother and was required to go in a closed sedan chair. When friends came to visit, she entertained them in her own apartment....

"At mealtimes men and women were separated. The men ate in a room just back of the reception hall, the women in one next to the kitchen. Men ate first, women next, and servants and slave girls last. Male guests were entertained in the reception hall by a man servant in the absence of the men of the family, until some of them got home.

"As small children, boys and girls played together, but after one of my brothers celebrated his ninth birthday he was no longer allowed to play as before with his sisters and female cousins. Although he might on occasion join in our activities, we saw him after that largely in a more formal way...." [11]

Childhood: The Beginning of Footbinding

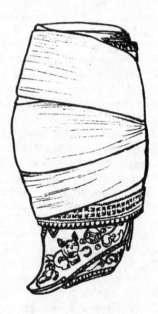

Bandaged foot and shoe

11. Suling Wang and Earl Herberg Cressy, *Daughter of Confucius* (New York: Farrar, Straus & Giroux, Inc., 1952), pp. 52–54.

The binding of women's feet in traditional China was such an important custom affecting women's lives that a separate essay deals more completely with this topic. However, since footbinding was started around the age of five or six it profoundly affected a Chinese girl's childhood.

Footbinding was a custom, dated from about the 11th century A.D., of very tightly wrapping a girl child's foot in long strips of cloth. The idea was to retard the growth of the feet, force the toes under the sole and the ball and heel of the foot together -- thus forming at adulthood tiny feet of three to five inches in length. Some members of all classes, gentry and peasant, bound their daughters' feet although it was more universal for the upper classes. Some tribal or minority peoples, like the Hakka of the southeastern mountains of China, resisted the custom. The higher class women probably had their feet bound more tightly than peasant women, but the ideal of tiny feet was almost universal in traditional China.

During the first year or two this bandaging was very painful. After this period of time the feet seemed to lose all feeling -- unless they were unbandaged, then pain returned. This account is by a Christian missionary to China around 1870. She overheard and went to investigate, the morning footbinding session of a small girl.

"I remember being greatly distressed one day by the crying of a child: 'O Auntie, Auntie, don't do so, it hurts; it hurts so much!' And then followed a long, quivering sobbing 'O-o-oh!' I tried not to mind it at first, and kept on with my writing for a little while, but I couldn't stand it very long-- the sobbing was too pitious. So I laid down my pen, put on my hat, and went round the corner into the alley where the sounds came from. It was dirty enough and narrow enough, I can assure you; but that was nothing. I only wanted to find out what could be the cause of this pitiful outcry, and what it was that 'auntie' was doing. So I pushed open the door that led into one of the courtyards, and there I saw how the matter stood. On a high bench, with her feet dangling half-way to the ground, sat a little girl about five years old, her face swollen with crying, and the tears pouring down her flushed cheeks; and nearby, seated in a chair, was that dreadful 'auntie,' a fat, middle aged woman who held one of the child's feet in her hand, while the other foot was hanging down bandaged very tight, and looking more like a large pear, tied round with blue cotton cloth, than a natural shaped foot. There the old auntie sat, with the other little bare foot in her hand, looking at it first on one side and then on the other, and particularly examining the parts where the little toes had been turned under and compressed by the bandages which had just been removed. She found these parts full of cracks and sores, and into these what do you think she put? Powdered saltpetre[12] to keep the sores from mortifying; and then she bound up the little foot again as tight as she could, and left the poor little sufferer with streaming eyes and dangling feet still sitting on the bench!"[13]

Besides the painful binding process, this custom meant that many Chinese girl's activities were limited by the crippling effects of the small bound feet. Domestic tasks, seclusion and bound feet all narrowed her childhood play.

12. Saltpetre of saltpeter (potassium nitrate or sodium nitrate). If applied to a wound or broken skin, this would hurt or sting. It also would not help the healing process.
13. Quoted in Rev. Ross C. Houghton, *Women of the Orient* (New York: Eaton & Mains, 1877), pp. 120-121.

Childhood: Selling a Girl Child

Another aspect of Chinese childhood especially for girls might be that they could be sold by their families. The next selection describes an aspect of this trade in children.

This incident took place in 1889 and is from an autobiography of a Chinese woman, Ning Lao Tai-tai. Her story was told to an American, Ida Pruitt, who lived in China in the 1930's and who became Ning Lao Tai-tai's friend.[14] In this selection Ning Lao Tai-tai described how her husband tried to sell their daughter and how she stopped the sale.

"One day when my husband handed the baby over to me as usual, saying, 'Nurse her,' one of the men in charge of the gruel[15] station saw him do it.

"'Is that your man?' said the man from the gruel station. I answered that he was.

"'He is trying to sell the child. He tells people that her mother died last Seventh Month.'

"'Oh, that is the talk that he uses for begging,' I said. But in my heart I wondered if it was true that he was trying to sell our child and to keep the knowledge from me.

"One day, when the ground was wet with melting snow, I found that even with the three pairs of shoes my feet were not covered. The bare flesh showed through.

"'You stay at home,' he said, 'and I will beg.' He took the child in his arms as usual. 'You wait at home,' he said. 'I will bring you food.'

"We waited, Manzi [the older daughter] and I. The day passed; it got dark; and still he did not come.... We lay in the dark. We had no lights that winter; we had no money for oil. I heard the watchman beating the third watch and I knew the night was half over. Still he did not come.

"Then I heard him push open the door and stumble as he crossed the threshold. He was opium sodden and uncertain in his movements. I waited for him to say as usual, 'Here, take the child and nurse her.' But there was no word. I heard him throwing something heavily on the bed....

"Then he struck a match and I saw that there was no child, only a bundle, a bundle of sweet potatoes.

"'I have sold her.'

"I jumped out of bed. I had no thought left for Manzi. I seized him by the queue [long braid]. I wrapped it three times around my arm. I fought him for my child. We rolled fighting on the ground.

"The neighbors came and talked to pacify us.

"'If the child has not left the city and we can keep hold of this one, we will find her,' they said.

"So we searched. The night through we searched. We went to the south city through the Drum Tower and back to the examination halls. We walked a great circle inside the city and always I walked with my hands on his queue. He could not get away.

"We found a house. The father of the child knocked. Some men came to the door. It was the house of dealers who buy up girls and sell them to brothels in other cities. Their trade is illegal, and if they are caught they are put in prison and punished. They dared not let me make a noise. I had but to cry aloud and the neighbors would be there. So the dealer in little girls said soft words. My neighbors said, 'What he says, he will do. Now that we have him we will find the child.' But the child was not in that house.

14. Ida Pruitt, from the story told her by Ning Lao Tai-tai, *A Daughter of Han* (Stanford, Ca: Yale University Press, 1945), pp. 66-69.
15. Thin cereal soup.

Family selling their little daughter during a famine in the 1920's. 65

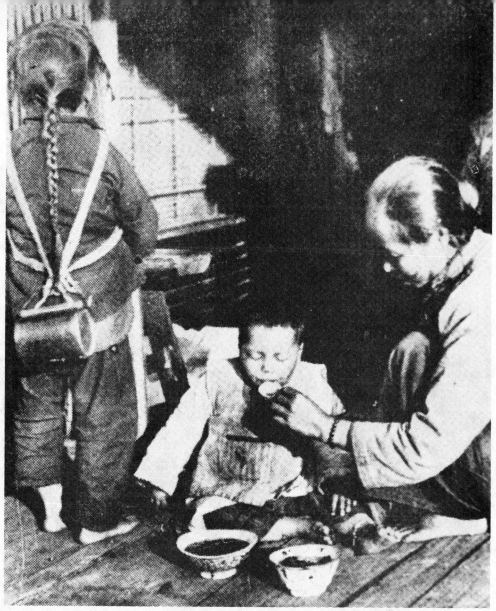

Boy child, on the left, with pigtail wears a tin can life preserver.

"'Take me to my child,' I demanded. The man promised. So again we started out in the night, walking and stumbling through the streets....

[The dealer in little girls takes the mother, Ning Lao Tai-tai, to another house.]

"The man who opened it held the two parts of the gate together with his hands to prevent anyone from going in. But I ducked under his arm before he could stop me and ran into the passage. I went through the courts, calling 'Jinya, Jinya.' The child heard my voice and knew me and answered, and so I found her. The woman of the house tried to hide the child behind her wide sleeves, but I pushed her aside and took the child into my arms. The man barred the door and said that I could not leave.

"'Then,' I said, 'I will stay here. My child is in my bosom. Mother and child, we will die here together.' I sat on the floor with my child in my arms." [16]

In this case Ning Lao Tai-tai was able to save her child for awhile. Many parents -- as the ones pictured in the photograph -- had to sell their daughters because of poverty.

Points To Consider

1. Why were girl babies usually considered to be the most expendable family members in traditional China? Under what conditions did a family desire a girl child? Under what conditions do you think both girl and boy infants might be destroyed at birth?

2. Why do you think infanticide was often used to control family size rather than other birth control methods? What conditions might have led to such a drastic solution to population control?

3. What specific things seem to indicate that boy and girl babies were handled alike? What specific things indicate a difference in treatment?

4. In 1908 a British naval officer related the following observation to an American woman traveler:

"...notice the next boat on the river which has children on it. You will see a log or a gourd tied around the waist of a male infant. This is so he can be hauled on board again in case he falls overboard. I defy you to ever see such a safety handle tied around the waist of a female infant." [17]

What have you studied that might support the truth of this observer's story? How might an historian question it?

5. What human relations skills might a young girl learn from being in charge of her even younger brothers and sisters?

6. Why might learning adult skills such as spinning and weaving be comparatively enjoyable for a young Chinese girl? What other activities might she have to do?

7. In what specific ways did the seclusion and segregation of the gentry girl seem difficult to you? In what ways quite comfortable?

8. Why do you think footbinding was started at such an early age? What made it so painful for this little girl?

9. Why did Ning Lao Tai-tai's husband try to sell their daughter? How did her mother, Ning Lao Tai-tai, get her back?

10. How might a parent justify the selling of their child?

16. Pruitt, pp. 66-69.
17. Mary Park Dunning, *Mrs. Marco Polo Remembers* (Boston: Houghton Mifflin Company, 1968), p. 29.

A. 2. Women As Young Adults

Betrothal:

In traditional China all adults were expected to be married. Although this requirement was common in many traditional peasant societies, for example in the Middle East and India, the marriage requirement was particularly strong in China because of the practice of "ancestor worship." Whether Chinese were Daoists, Buddhists or worshipped local folk deities, they all seemed to have followed the rites of ancestor worship.

Central to the practice of ancestor worship was the notion of a continuation of each family by the sons of each generation. The sons watched over their elderly parents, provided elaborate and proper funerals upon their deaths and performed the rites that would assure the immortality of the dead souls. Perhaps a universal human motive for having children is so that parents can be linked to the past and future through their children. For the Chinese this idea was formulated into a fixed belief that without the son (and son's son down through the generations), the souls of the dead would cease to exist. In this system of belief, time is measured not in terms of one span of life, but as a continuing and possibly never ending chain of generations.

Perhaps the practice of ancestor worship developed from Confucian ideals of "filial piety" --the absolute obedience to and reverence of sons and daughters for their parents or for

adult women's obedience to their parents-in-law. Possibly this formal system of giving complete devotion to parents both in this life and after their deaths came from the insecurity of Chinese peasant life. So many catastrophes or disasters occurred periodically in parts of China-- floods, droughts, attacks from foreign enemies, plagues-- that the following of this rigid set of rules and rites might have provided security and hope of continuity to people. Whatever the origin of these practices, the necessity of ancestor worship by sons meant that marriage was an absolute requirement.

It was not the young people's task to find a marriage partner. All marriages were arranged by the parents, usually by the mother. The parents were helped by a "go between" or matchmaker who tried to find an appropriate bride or groom and negotiated the terms of the marriage. This search for a correct mate might start almost at the child's birth-- sometimes even before it was born. Occasionally, two families would agree that if the proper sex of child was born to each that they would betroth their children at birth.

Why was there this frantic search for marriage partners for children? The process of finding a bride or groom was often a complicated one:

--- It was illegal to marry any person with the same surname. Since many villages were made up of all one clan with the same surname, the search had to be carried on outside the village. Even in villages composed of more than one clan, it was considered a mistake to marry within the village.

--- There were economic and social considerations-- families should be of about the same wealth and status.

--- A bride price had to be saved by the groom's family and paid to the family of the bride at the time of the marriage.

--- The bride's family was usually expected to provide a dowry of household goods, though this was usually considerably less than the bride price.

--- Because of the neglect of female babies and female infanticide, there was a much higher death rate among female infants than male. This caused an imbalance of more young men than young women in the population. Because of the comparative scarcity of women, women became more valuable as families looked for brides for their sons.

When parents debated the merits of various potential marriage partners for their sons and daughters, they usually did not consider the feelings or preferences of the young people. However, they might consider some personal characteristics, especially of the future son-in-law in making their choice. A daughter-in-law was usually picked for her good health (so she could have children), skills in domestic work and a "good reputation" -- meaning she was obedient to her parents and had had no love affairs. Different requirements were looked for in a son-in-law for a daughter. Martin Yang, who studied a village in Shantung before World War II, described how peasants in this village picked future husbands for their daughters:

"In choosing a family for one's daughter... the parents' first consideration is the economic condition of the family-- how much land and how many houses the family owns. The girl's mother finds out how many sons the family has and calculates how much each one of the brothers will have when the property is finally divided. It makes a great difference when one compares a family that has twenty mou of land but only one son, with one that has thirty mou but three sons.

"If the economic condition is satisfactory, the mother will take the boy's personal qualifications into consideration, but will not make too much fuss about this. It is a strong rather than a handsome body that matters. A pockmarked face will not matter if everything else is all right. Careful mothers also pay attention to the boy's personality. The moral standard for a man is different from that for a woman. He is not strictly subjected to sexual morality, to conventional manners, to domestic regulations as a woman is, but if he is known to be hot-tempered, or to have unpopular habits, such as drinking, smoking, or gambling, the chances for marriage will be lessened." [1]

When the parents have decided on a marriage partner for their son or daughter, the formal betrothal takes place. Though customs varied somewhat at different times and places, Martin Yang's description of this process seems representative of engagements in traditional China. [2]

Formal request:
"When the two families are satisfied [by the negotiations], a formal letter is sent by the boy's family in which the engagement of the girl to the boy is requested."

1. Martin Yang, *A Chinese Village, Daidon Shandong Province* (New York: Columbia University Press, 1945), pp. 107-108.

2. *Ibid.*, p. 108.

Gifts:
"[The letter] is accompanied by presents to the girl's parents. Generally, these consist of forty big steamed rolls, made of refined wheat flour, a large piece of pork (about 15 pounds, or less), and several kinds of cakes. The girl receives jewelry, dress material, money, and other articles useful to the bride, the amount and quality varying according to the economic condition of the boy's family."

Money:
"In some cases a sum of money...is also given to the girl's parents.... When a girl is to be engaged to a boy who has a lot of brothers, or whose family is not well-to-do, the girl's parents will drive a hard bargain and demand as much money or goods as possible for the girl."

Selling the Daughter:
"Occasionally, however, some of [the money] will be spent by her father for the family's livelihood [instead of on the bride's trousseau]. This would make the parents unpopular, and fellow villagers would say that they are selling their daughter."

Engagement:
"The engagement ceremony takes place at the girl's home. In most cases, the boy's father, or a person who can act in the father's place, presents the letter and gifts. The girl's parents formally entertain the guest. Senior members among the close relatives are invited to the party."

Acknowledgement of New Relationship:
"From this time on, the two families are relatives and address each other with the proper terms."

Public Announcements:
"Both families announce the engagement by distributing the big rolls to relatives, friends, and neighbors."

Sometimes betrothals were arranged

between young children-- occasionally even infants-- especially among the gentry class. In these cases several years would go by before the wedding. It was expected that the families of the future bride and groom, and particularly the engaged couple, would avoid each other. Since the young woman was kept close at home, or even secluded, and the couple would probably be from different villages, it was not likely that they would meet. Among poor peasants the young man might have difficulty finding a bride. He might be comparatively old and the wedding could take place almost immediately after the engagement. How binding was the betrothal? There seems to be some disagreement among various observers. Some say that it was not final, but would have been embarrassing to the families if the engagement was broken. Other sources indicate that it was quite a final step and a betrothal was only broken in the most unusual circumstances. It is likely that the families did take the betrothal of their children very seriously. In China these were family affairs, involving money and family honor-- not an agreement between two young people. Chinese values emphasized the family, not the individual's desires. Marriage was considered too important to the group's security to leave it to an individual's choice. But for the women in the family it was a particularly important time. The mothers of the bride and groom had played crucial roles in the negotiations and their status rose with the betrothal of their children. For the engaged daughter it was a time when her value as a person was recognized by both families. However, her future was largely decided by others.

Points To Consider

1. Briefly describe the Chinese belief and practice of ancestor worship. Why did these practices make marriage so important?

2. What things made it particularly difficult for the family of a poor man to find a bride for him?

3. What considerations were taken into account when selecting a son-in-law for a daughter? When selecting a daughter-in-law?

4. What do you think were reasons for all the customs and ceremonies surrounding a traditional Chinese betrothal? Why might they be so difficult to dissolve even when the betrothal took place years before the wedding?

Wedding:

Virtually all writers about social life in traditional China devote space to lengthy descriptions of Chinese weddings. Christian missionaries, travelers, officials of foreign governments and, more recently, social scientists all seem to have felt compelled to write about them. What characteristics might have made Chinese weddings so fascinating to various observers?

--- They were very public affairs; much of the celebrating and feasting was carried on where anyone could at least be an observer.

--- For the Western foreigner to China they were quite different from weddings in Europe or America, so seemed exotic and strange.

--- Perhaps more than in any other society, the wedding marked the most dramatic changes in the life of a bride. To talk about women in China, observers felt that it was necessary to describe this important ceremony.

Wedding: Teasing the Bride

Seemingly a standard part of a Chinese wedding was something called "teasing the bride." However, various observers have written about this custom differently. Here are four versions-- as you read them, note the differences in these versions of the same custom.

1. Lin Yaohua, a Chinese sociologist who wrote a novel about life in a Chinese village in the early 20th century:

"Most of the guests dispersed after dinner, but a few young men rushed to the bridal room in order to 'tease the bride' as the custom went, their object being to make the bride laugh by all sorts of jokes, and to submit the bride and groom to all kinds of merry embarrassment. At long last they left, but not till the bride had

bribed them with the gift of some of her handkerchiefs."[1]

2. Francis L. K. Xu, a Chinese social scientist writing at about the same time as Lin, describes the teasing this way:

"On the wedding day the main interest is provided by the bride. Everybody except the elderly males, wants to have a peep at her; she sits practically motionless all day long, except when told to partake of food ceremonially with the bridegroom. At dusk the fervor centering around the bride runs even higher. The younger people, male and female, crowd into the bride and bridegroom's new room and make fun of them. The couple are compelled to perform stunts, to make gestures of intimacy, and so forth. And the merriment infects everyone present. It lasts until about midnight, and then the guests disperse after yet another meal, consisting of noodles, preserved sweets, peanuts, and tea."[2]

1. Lin Yaohua, *The Golden Wing* (London: Kegan Paul, Trench, Trubner & Co., 1948), p. 47.
2. Francis L. K. Xu, *Under the Ancestor's Shadow* (Stanford, CA: Stanford University Press, 1967), pp. 97-98. This book is a later edition of his 1948 book.

A nineteenth century wedding in China.

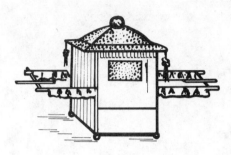

Bridal sedan chair

3. Justus Doolittle, Christian missionary to China in the mid-1800's, describes this teasing this way:

"According to another established custom here, except in the case of marriages in the families of officers and the gentry, neighbors, uninvited friends, or even perfect strangers to the parties, if they please, are allowed to come in and see the bride during the evening of the day of her marriage. This is a very trying ordeal for her, as she may not refuse to be seen by them, nor absent herself from the gaze of the public. She is obliged to stand while a company of spectators observes her appearance and criticizes her deportment. They indulge oftentimes in great liberty of remark about her, which she must bear with composure. What at other times would be likely to be regarded as insulting and highly indecent, must be passed over as though she heard it not. Should she allow herself to laugh, or should she forget herself enough to manifest anger, it would be a source of annoyance and of regret. Her husband generally absents himself from the public room during this evening. It not unfrequently occurs that some of his intimate friends or neighbors stay very late, refusing to depart unless he pledges them a considerable sum of money with which to pay the expenses of a feast on the following day."[3]

4. Mary Isabella Bryson, a British missionary in the late 19th century, gave the following description of the teasing:

"It is indeed a trying ordeal for the girl bride, for the wedding guests are allowed to indulge in all kinds of uncomplimentary criticisms as to her personal appearance. During this annoying experience, which lasts sometimes for two days or more, the poor young bride must listen with immovable features to all the various verdicts of praise or blame which the numerous guests care to pronounce upon her. Poor child!"[4]

Points To Consider

1. What specific differences do you notice between these four accounts? What reasons might there be for these differences?

2. Justus Doolittle's and Isabella Bryson's accounts describe the teasing as an "ordeal" for the bride. Why do they see this as a difficult ordeal? Might an historian have some doubts or questions about their description of the teasing? Why? What might make their accounts fairly reliable?

3. This teasing might be compared to the hazing of first year students at West Point or of Marine recruits. Depending on which version you believe, what purposes might there be to this "teasing of the bride?"

4. What kinds of teasing sometimes goes on at American weddings? What do you see as the purposes of this teasing?

3. Justus Doolittle, *Social Life of the Chinese* (London: Sampson, Low Son and Marston, 1868), pp. 63–64.
4. Mary Isabella Bryson, *The Land of the Pigtail* (London: Sunday School Union, n.d.), p. 83.

Nineteenth century village woman and sons.

Motherhood:

Traditional Chinese women had almost no status in the family into which they had married until they gave birth to their first child-- preferably a son. This was true of both peasant and gentry women. After a woman became pregnant she was given more consideration, though if she was a peasant woman she continued to work hard through her pregnancy.

If the young mother were from the gentry class the birth of her first baby would have been accompanied by ceremony and joy-- especially if the baby was a boy. The following is a selection from an account of an American Quaker woman, Nora Waln, who lived with a Chinese gentry family for awhile in the 1930's. She described the birth of a son to a family daughter-in-law:

"...The child entered the world at dawn on the Birthday of the Sun, after distress, alarm, and delay so prolonged that the Family Elders had met in the Hall of Ancestors to consider the wisdom of sending to Peking for a Western-educated woman doctor to assist.

"For a day and a night of Soumai's pain, her husband waited before her door. As Mai-da and I were dispatched here and there to various parts of the homestead on errands for the women who attended Soumai, we were awed by his stillness. He stood hour after hour, refusing to sit or to partake of refreshment, clutching a fold of his grey gown in the fingers of one hand.

"Then when Soumai's mother came to the door, just as the sun rose, and announced, 'A man is born,' he disappeared. He returned some time later dressed in his ceremonial robes. After another long wait at the door his mother opened it and told him to come in.

"Soumai was wrapped in the robe of apple-blossom silk which was her marriage-bed nightdress. She held the child against her breast. I saw her smile as her husband came near to her.

"Before he took the child she offered, or looked on its face, he put on her pillow, as thanks-gift, a gold hairpin such as each mother of a son wears in her nape knot. In his wife's pin he had set an oblong of clear green jade.

"Then he took the child in its warm wrappings of rosy satin in the palms of his two hands. He knelt to his own mother. He knelt to his wife's mother. He carried his son through every court in the homestead, making the new Lin's arrival known, with ceremony, to all the Family-- men, women, and children-- and to the God of the Hearth. Standing under the lamp of continuous life, he told the glad tidings in the Hall of the Ancestors.

"Then he gave his son back into his wife's keeping for the 'three days of quietness,' when her own mother and her serving woman, Little Tiger, were the only persons permitted to enter the court of her dwelling...."[1]

With the birth of a first, healthy baby -- especially a son-- the Chinese woman's status began to improve within the joint family. She was now a mother and by the laws of "filial piety" her sons and daughters would owe her as much respect as they owed their father. If her child was a boy, she would be included on the family tablet at the ancestor altar after her death. If the first child were a daughter the excitement was present, but more reserved. The "sao chu" or "three day" ceremony took place a few days after the baby's birth and usually marked only the first child's birth. The celebration was held whether the baby was a boy or a girl, but was probably more elaborate for a boy.[2]

1. Nora Waln, *The House of Exile* (Boston: Little Brown and Company, 1933), pp. 83-84.
2. Francis L. K. Xu, *Under the Ancestor's Shadow* (Stanford, CA: Stanford University Press, 1967), pp. 198-199.

Mother pushing baby for a stroll.

If time went by and a woman did not have a baby, this became a terrible misery for her. A barren or childless woman in traditional China was considered quite worthless. The following is a description written in the mid–1800's by a missionary to China of some of the strange or desperate measures these barren women would resort to in order to assure a pregnancy:

"When the woman has been married for a long time, but remains childless, the following expedient is sometimes adopted. A girl belonging to another family is adopted by the childless woman as her own child. She is brought up in her family, and treated as though she was her own child. The Chinese have the idea that, in some way, this course will aid the woman in the conception of children. The train of thought is explained thus: The woman is represented by a tree in the unseen world. Whether she will have children or not, and what will be their number and sex, is indicated by the condition of the tree which represents her, whether it has flowers or not;...if no flowers at all, the poor woman will not naturally have any children at all. But as, in this world, men graft one tree by a shoot of another tree, and thus have the desired fruit, the Chinese have devised the idea of adopting a child into a childless family, hoping that thus there will in due time be flowers on the flowerless tree in the spirit land, representing the barren wife;

Mother and child in China today.

and if so, she will be sure to have children, in consequence of this wonderful art of grafting.

"Sometimes the childless married woman hires a sorceress, who pretends to be able to see into the other world, to examine the flower-tree which represents her, and to report to her its condition, whether it is flourishing or whether it is diseased, what flowers it has, and whether the red or white flowers will probably blossom first.

"Every year, between the 11th and the 15th of the first and of the eighth Chinese months, several of the most popular temples devoted to the worship of a goddess of children, commonly called 'Mother,' are frequented by married but childless women, for the purpose of procuring one of a kind of shoe belonging to her. Those who come for a shoe burn incense and candles before the image of 'Mother,' and vow to render a thanksgiving if she will aid them in bearing a male child. The shoe is taken home, and placed in the niche or by the niche which holds the family image of the goddess.... When the child thus prayed for is born, should such a fortunate event take place, the happy mother causes, according to her vow, two shoes like the one obtained from the temple to be made."[3]

The desperation of a Chinese wife to have living male children meant that women who were not barren usually tried to have all the children they could. For them one pregnancy often follows another. Death in childbirth of mother or baby was common and the mother became ill or worn out from the frequent pregnancies and strenuous task of caring for her babies. Gentry women had servants and "wet nurses" to care for their babies, but peasant women could not even afford to rest a few days after the births of their babies. A peasant woman might depend on her older children to watch her babies.

However, no matter how much these children were wanted, the burdens of childbirth and raising large families made life very difficult for these peasant women.

Points To Consider

1. Why might it be all right if the first child was a girl? However, what specific things in these accounts indicate that it was a much happier occasion if the first born was a boy?

2. Why did women in traditional China generally try to have as many children as possible?

3. What do you think might have happened to a woman who seemed to be barren?

3. Justus Doolittle, *Social Life of the Chinese* (London: Sampson Low Son and Marston, 1869), pp. 81–83.

A. 3. Women in Old Age

"Old Age" in China was considered to begin at about age forty. Though generally "old age" was considered desirable and the elderly were respected, other factors also influenced a person's status.

In traditional China everyone's status depended on these categories:

Occupation or Class:

Highest	Scholar-official
	Peasant farmer
	Merchant
Lowest	Soldier

Sex:

Highest	Male
Lowest	Female

Generation:[1]

Highest	Grandparents
	Parents
Lowest	Unmarried children

Age:

Highest	Older
Lowest	Younger

In traditional China an individual's status might have depended on some additional factors:

Man

Intellectual ability-- to pass standard exams meant official recognition as a "scholar" of several grades which meant appointments to prized government jobs.

Family size-- number of sons that would share in the family property; eldest son got an extra share, but otherwise property was divided evenly.

Type of wealth-- inherited land was considered to bring more prestige than business income.

Woman

Giving birth to a son-- or sons; being a mother of daughters only or barren.

Personality-- her ability to dominate or submit to the family she married into could make her local reputation.

Personal property-- a woman was allowed to keep jewelry, clothing, individual savings and money earned strictly on her own time. The evidence from traditional China suggests that few women owned personal property of any significance nor were they usually able to earn money outside the family.[2]

1. Generation took precedence over Age. For example, if a woman was married to the eldest son of a family she would have more status than the wife of the younger son even though the eldest's son's wife was younger than the other wife.

2. For an argument that some women on Taiwan control quite a bit of property see: Myron Cohen, *House United, House Divided* (New York: Columbia University Press, 1976). For suggestion that in traditional China this was usually of limited significance see: C. K. Yang, *A Chinese Village in Early Communist Transition* (Cambridge, Massachusetts, MIT Press, 1959), p. 90.

Three generations of modern Chinese women.

Though a man's status increased with old age, a woman's status increased more dramatically with age because she had had the lowest status in the household as a young bride and daughter-in-law. To improve her position substantially she had to have at least one male child. It was when her son married and she became a mother-in-law and finally a grandmother that she could achieve both power and honor within the family. Some observers feel that occasionally these older Chinese women achieved an absolute hold over their families:

"The authority of the mother was second only to that of the father. If her husband were dead the dowager of the eldest generation reigned almost supreme. The authority of the old woman of position in China is a thing which defies definition. It has been said that the strongest title to a piece of land in China is that of an old woman occupying it who refuses to get off. Almost anyone else can be dispossessed, but the combination of the dowager's actual helplessness with the veneration [respect] given to age, plus the importance of public opinion in China, make it almost

impossible to dispossess her. Such old women do practically as they please."[3]

Not only her authority, but a woman's emotional ties might be more secure in old age. An older woman would probably continue to have a close relationship with her son, even after he married. She might jealously guard this relationship against the competition with her daughter-in-law. She possibly would now have a closer and friendlier relationship with her husband because of mutual sharing of work and family responsibilities over the years. However, the anthropologist, Francis Xu, points out that this possibly closer relationship of the older couple probably did not include sexual intimacy:

"...We have seen the intense desire for sons. Yet in West Town,...there is a practice which must by any definition be considered as birth control. Husbands and wives sleep in the same room as long as their sons are not married. After the latter's marriage, some parents continue to sleep in the same room; others do not. After the birth of a grandchild, it is definitely more desirable for the older couple to live in different rooms; it would be considered disgraceful for the older woman to become pregnant after such an event.

"A review of the family cases investigated shows that with few exceptions old couples whose married sons have children live separately. In a family, which keeps two small dry goods stores, the parents have four sons, only one of whom was not married at the time of this investigation. The old father sleeps in the shop on one side of the street, while the old mother sleeps in the one on the opposite side of the street....

"In discussing this matter West Towners uniformly gave me the following reasons: 'It looks

embarrassing for a couple to sleep together after their son is married,' or 'It is shameful for a woman to get pregnant after her daughter-in-law has already entered the house."[4]

As the daughter-in-law had now entered the family, the duty of carrying on the family line was hers. This meant that for many Chinese women old age was their happiest life stage:[5]

--- They had finally achieved high status within the family.

--- They might have to work less and had time for such activities as religion, matchmaking, friendships and even gambling.

--- They often spent much time with their grandchildren and were useful as sitters without the responsibilities of being a parent.

--- Unlike younger women, they could appear at public gatherings, smoke in public and be outspoken in their opinions.[6] They seemed released from the male domination that ruled their lives until old age.

Of course, old age also brought the discomforts of disease or infirmity to many elderly people. This next excerpt is told by an American doctor, Ruth Hemenway, who organized a hospital in China in the 1920's. The incident shows something of both the toughness of this grandmother and the devotion given to the elderly by the younger family members, in this case a grandson:

3. Herrlee Glessner Creel, *The Birth of China* (New York: Frederick Ungar Publishers, 1937), p. 302.

4. Francis L. K. Xu, *Under the Ancestor's Shadow*, pp. 109–110.

5. For a description of the activities of elderly women see: Margery Wolf, *Women and the Family in Rural Taiwan* (Stanford, CA: Stanford University Press, 1972), pp. 215–229.

6. Bernard Gallin, *Xin Xing, Taiwan* (Berkeley, CA: University of California Press, 1966), p. 215. Although Wolf's and Gallin's studies were of modern Taiwan, old age may have been much the same in traditional China.

82 **Older women in China sometimes had more opportunity for rest.**

"Dr. Dang and I went to the front gate and found a weary little old lady sitting on the sawhorse which served as the gateboy's seat. We inquired about her health and whether she had eaten. Then we asked, 'Have you come a long distance?'

"'Three days' journey. Three days' journey.' she said proudly in her quavering old voice. Three days of walking on tiny bound feet in red embroidered cloth shoes. Three days of walking along narrow, stonepaved trails with one hand holding the shoulder of her ten year old grandson who had walked a pace ahead of her. Three days on her poor, aching bound feet; up and down steep stairs over the mountains; across swaying bridges over the roaring mountain streams. I tried to think what it must have been like for both of them.

"'Can my eyes be repaired?' she asked eagerly. She had severe trachoma [an eye disease]. The inflammation had inverted the eyelids until the lashes were rubbing constantly on the balls of her eyes. This constant irritation had caused swelling, blurred vision, and finally complete blindness.

"'We can cure your eyes if you are willing to let us open the knife,' we told her.

"Her stalwart young grandson standing beside her looked anxiously at her. 'She is too old,' he protested. 'She cannot endure to have her eyes cut.'

"But grandmother spoke up for herself. 'I am old and without eyes. I am no good. I prefer to let the doctor open the knife.'

"It was a simple matter to clear up the trachoma. Then we cut out a piece of flesh from under each lower lid and stitched the cut edges together. This pulled out the eyelid and made the lashes point outward, thus relieving the irritation.... In a few days the old lady began to see a little. When the day came for her to return home, the whole staff stood under the camphor tree to say goodbye. We watched her trip off happily upriver toward her home.... No longer did she have to keep her hand on her manly little grandson's shoulder."[7]

A granddaughter might also feel close to a grandmother— and sometimes be granted special privileges not allowed other family members. The next description is of a grandmother who organized and directed a large and wealthy gentry household.

"After my personal slave girl, my earliest recollections center around my grandmother, whose energetic presence dominated these inner apartments and who indeed had virtually ruled over our branch of the clan since the death of my grandfather when I was four....

"Grandmother would stalk into a room and give a keen glance around. She missed nothing. All present would rise to greet her.

"'Good morning, grandmother,' the members of the family would say, and the servants and slave girls would echo, 'Good morning, Lao Tai Tai,' which means 'old lady' but carries the respectful meaning of elder or venerable lady....

"She was so fat that no chair in the house was wide enough for her to sit down. Therefore, when she visited the rooms of the various ladies of our household, she sat on benches with two slave girls standing behind her serving her tea, fanning her, or holding the little gray monkey that First Uncle had brought her from Java and that was her special pet. Most of the time, however, she used a rattan chair which was moved from place to place. When I think of her, I

7. Ruth Hemenway, *A Memoir of Revolutionary China, 1924-1941* (Amherst, MA: University of Massachusetts Press, 1977), pp. 34–35.

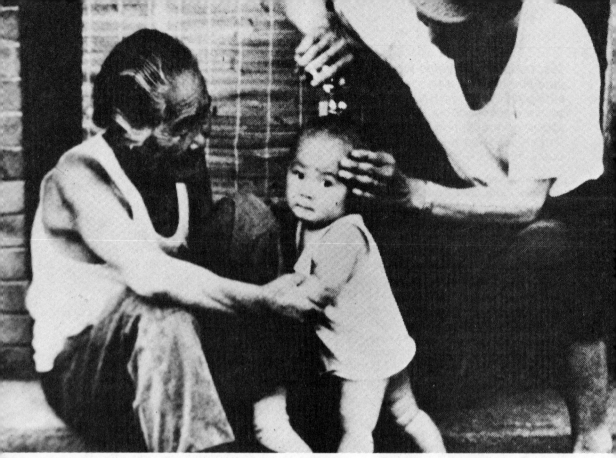

Grandmother helping with her grandchild's hair cut

see her with her two slave girls, one on each side, tugging at her arms and helping her heave herself up out of this chair.

"As her youngest granddaughter, and daughter of her favorite son, I was in a special position. She seemed to like to have me around, and would ask, 'Where is Aling... hah... why isn't she here with me?'

[One afternoon] Grandmother was in an unofficial mood for the moment, leisurely sipping tea.... The two little black dogs played beside her, and on her knee sat the little gray monkey....

"I was leaning against grandmother's knee, patting her hands and reaching my hand up her wide sleeves. I loved doing this, and she seemed to like to have me do it, although none of the

rest of our family ventured on such familiarity. As Jem Po [the slave girl] passed the cakes I took one and offered it to the Little Man, who stood up politely to take it. When he finished the cake he sat down again to scratch his ribs. At this point an idea was born. I took hold of the monkey gently and thrust him swiftly just as far as I could reach up grandmother's wide sleeve.

"At once there ensued the greatest clawing, chattering, and snorting. Grandmother, with a convulsive movement of her arm, swept the Little Man out of her sleeve onto the ground. There was first a gray streak as the monkey flashed up grandmother's knee and onto her shoulder, and then a red streak as I dived for the shelter of the nearest pot of peonies, from where I looked out cautiously. The mingled snorting and chattering continued as grandmother and her little monkey voiced their combined surprise and indignation. All the onlookers held their breath.

"Grandmother turned from soothing the monkey, and glared at me indignantly.

"'Impudent small devil... hah...' she snorted. I began to fear the worst.

"'Come here, Aling... hah...' she commanded, and I obeyed as she turned again to the little monkey and began to smooth his ruffled fur.

"The others let out their breath and Orchid Blossom moved forward to take me away.

"'Let her stay... hah...' said grandmother.

"From that time on I was regarded among the children in our household with respect and given the nickname of Dan Da. This is an adjective in common use and means literally 'great gall.' Looking back, I think the reason I was able to act this way and live to tell the tale was that I was not afraid of her.... I sensed, behind her austere manner, a kindliness she was forced to cover up in order to maintain her place as virtual ruler of the eighty persons who made up our household...although I could not fully realize the difficulty of one woman maintaining the order and discipline of our big household and the strain it put on her. It was perhaps this knowledge we shared in common,... that made me her favorite grandchild."[8]

Points To Consider

1. In our culture, women, especially, have been known to lie about how old they are and it is considered rude to ask older people their age. In traditional China older women and men were proud of their advancing years. It was considered a compliment to call someone "old."

   A. In what specific ways was it an advantage to be an old person in traditional China compared to earlier stages of life? Why was aging especially an advantage for women?

   B. List some reasons why you think Americans are often ashamed or fearful of aging. Why do you think the Chinese did not admire youth in their culture they way we do in ours?

   C. Do you see some value in the way the Chinese treated older people? Why or why not?

   D. When do you consider that someone enters old age?

2. Why might a custom develop that separated a husband and wife after the marriage of their children?

3. Why do you think the grandson and grandmother were so determined to make the very difficult trip to get the grandmother's eyes treated? What things impressed you about their story?

4. In the excerpt about the gentry family:

   A. How would you describe Aling's grandmother?

   B. Why do you think the grandmother had become the leader of this large family?

   C. Why do you think the granddaughter, Aling, could get away with the practical joke of putting the monkey up the grandmother's sleeve?

8. Wong Suling and Earl Herbert Cressy, *Daughter of Confucius* (New York: Farrar Straus and Young, 1952), pp. 11–18.

B. Mother-in-law/ Daughter-in-law: Women As Family Adversaries

"...The completion of the marriage day's ceremonies might be said to have taken place the following morning. At that time the new bride arose early and went to the rooms of her new parents. She took them morning tea and breakfast and waited upon her mother-in-law that she might comb her mother-in-law's hair and do her bidding. This performance in a sense marked the true conclusion of the marriage ceremony and the beginning of her normal career as daughter-in-law."[1]

The Chinese mother-in-law in the traditional Chinese joint family has been characterized as a harsh, often cruel disciplinarian and taskmistress of her daughter-in-law. It appears that this is not a mere stereotype as there is abundant evidence that supports the view that the Chinese mother-in-law tyrannized her daughter-in-law. In fact, in few other cultures is the mother-in-law/ daughter-in-law relationship discussed so frequently and in such bleak terms as it is in traditional China.

The following information deals with the mother-in-law/daughter-in-law relationship in traditional China. Do the exercises on pages 87 and 88 as a group or as individuals.

Daughter-in-law

1. Probably she was quite young-- between 14 and 18 when she married.

2. Upon marriage, she left her natal[2] home to live with her husband's family.

3. Almost always her new home was in another village.

4. Until marriage she was kept close to home, perhaps secluded, and rarely given a formal education.

5. She may have been taught some skills at home-- domestic arts or spinning and weaving-- that she could contribute to her new family's welfare. However, there was little motivation for her natal family to have her educated or trained. A Chinese proverb said:
   "Daughters are born facing out"... meaning that they soon married and moved away.

6. She had probably been in charge of younger children since she was a small child. She may have learned to "boss" and manipulate younger brothers or sisters to make them do what she wanted.

---

1. Marion Levy, *The Family Revolution in Modern China* (New York: Atheneum, 1968), p. 105.
2. Natal means birth -- so, her home where she was born.

7. Her natal family probably had required a great deal of work from her. A common nickname in parts of China for young girls was "Yatou"... "slave girl."

8. After marriage her husband's family had the right to all her labor. She was not to visit her natal home without permission.

9. It was considered to be unfilial for her husband to take her side in arguments with his mother. He was not to show any signs of affection or interest toward her in front of other family members.

10. She was absolutely under the command of her mother-in-law. By custom the ideal daughter-in-law was completely submissive and did the bidding of her mother-in-law without question.

11. If she died before she gave birth to a son, her name was not included on the family ancestor's tablet. It was as if she had never existed.

12. She probably had never seen her husband until their wedding day. Her parents had arranged her marriage.

13. Marriages in China were arranged between families-- not individuals. Therefore, a new bond may have been formed between the two families/ clans by the marriage. In times of need families connected by marriage often helped each other by supplying labor or loans. If her natal family heard she was badly abused, they might be unhappy and might come to help her or refuse aid to her new family if they fell on hard times.

14. She was supposed to be more interested in the comfort of her parents-in-law than in her own or her husband's comfort.

Mother-in-law

15. She had been a daughter-in-law.

16. Her status had risen because:
-- she had given birth to at least one son

-- she had arranged a marriage for this son
-- she was now older

17. If she was a peasant, she had worked very hard during her years of marriage raising her children. Also, she had given birth to them under very difficult circumstances.

18. She probably was not particularly close to her husband, although they may have gained respect for each other through years of labor and having children together.

19. Her main emotional ties were with her sons. Their births had brought her some relief from the complete tyranny of her mother-in-law and had raised her status.

20. After babyhood, the father was expected to be very remote and rather harsh toward his sons. She, the mother, became their confidant and support.

21. By custom she was expected to be distant and harsh to her daughter-in-law. She could even discipline her by using physical punishment.

22. She lost face if she was very nice to her daughter-in-law or complimented her too often.

23. She lost face if it became known that her daughter-in-law was very badly treated-- especially if the daughter-in-law committed suicide because of ill treatment.

Group Exercise

Select a recorder and then record your group's answers to the problems below.

1) Each item of information has a number before it. On the work sheet or a piece of paper list the numbers that apply to Part A and Part B.

   A. Daughters-in-law: List the weapons or advantages that daughters-in-law could use to protect their interests in their new family and try to control their mothers-in-law.

B. Mothers-in-law: List the weapons or advantages that mothers-in-law could use to protect their interests and try to control their daughters-in-law.

2) Discuss what you as a group think was the most powerful advantage of: A. the daughters-in-law B. the mothers-in-law. After you have made your decisions, jot down your two selections and a few reasons for your choices.

3) It might be supposed that having been treated harshly or even cruelly when she was a daughter-in-law a woman might be a kind mother-in-law. The evidence shows that this is not the case in traditional China. Why would a woman who was once a daughter-in-law be a harsh mother-in-law?

A. Practical or economic reasons:

B. Psychological or emotional reasons:

4) Each group member rank the following things about being a daughter-in-law in China that might have bothered you the most (1 to 10). As a group, discuss your first and last choices. Can you agree on the worst aspects?

To obey all the wishes and commands of your mother-in-law.

Not to know your husband before your wedding day.

To have to move away from your family home and village.

To be expected to be up the earliest and work the hardest of any female family member.

To be expected to submit without protest to physical or verbal abuse from your mother-in-law.

To have your husband ignore you except when you were alone.

To have your husband take his mother's side in arguments between you and her.

To feel you must become pregnant and have a son as soon as possible.

Not to be able to visit your home or family without your mother-in-law's permission.

5) This section is called "Mother-in-law/Daughter-in-law: Women As Family Adversaries". If we were writing about an American marriage the title would probably be "Marriage: Wife and Husband."

A. Why was the title "Mother-in-law/Daughter-in-law: Women As Family Adversaries"?

B. What does your group think were the main purposes of marriage in traditional China? What are the main purposes of marriage in your country?

C. What problems might a young traditional Chinese husband encounter in trying to maintain a peaceful household atmosphere?

C. Family Tensions and the Daughter-in-law

As the preceding exercise might suggest, there were many reasons why the mother–in–law and daughter–in–law in a traditional Chinese family rarely, sincerely liked each other. A multitude of sources–– both Chinese and foreign–– agree that the daughter–in–law/mother–in–law relationship in the joint family of traditional China was almost always an unhappy one. Occasionally, a mother-in-law would genuinely like her daughter–in–law and it would seem that conflict between the two women might be avoided. However, even when the relationship started as a friendly one it usually cooled with time. This may have been normal consequences of living and working so closely together, competing for the affection of the son and the comparatively powerless position of the daughter-in-law. An anthropologist studying in modern Taiwan observed another pressure on this relationship between daughter-in-law and mother-in-law:

"...When one village woman praised her new daughter-in-law repeatedly the situation was so widely discussed that references to the matter appear again and again in my notes over a period of several months. At first the tone of the village response was one of knowing amusement, everyone confidently implying that it would not last more than a few weeks. When the usual change for the worse did not take place quite as soon as expected, this attitude gradually gave *way to resentment and even irritation. Several women felt that the mother-in-law in question was causing everyone trouble by praising her daughter-in-law. As one of them explained, 'She just goes round telling everyone how good her daughter-in-law is and this makes a lot of trouble. It makes others angry at their own daughters-in-law just to hear it.' The eventual deterioration of the relationship was greeted by the family's relatives and neighbors with satisfaction and relief."[1]*

The sources also agree that the daughter-in-law was often treated cruelly. She was expected to work hard, to be affectionate and to be obedient to her parents-in-law and to submit passively to criticism and even physical punishment. There were no institutional controls such as government or church laws that she could turn to for support against abusive treatment. Her main protection against unfair or harsh punishment were her own natal family and clan support and her own determination.

If her natal family found out she was being badly abused or physically harmed by her mother-in-law or new family they might interfere. However,

1. Arthur P. Wolf, "Adopt a Daughter-in-law, Marry a Sister: A Chinese Solution to the Problem of the Incest Taboo," *American Anthropolotist,* Vol. 70 (1968), p. 869. Taiwan still keeps to many of the customs of traditional China.

the abuse had to be severe before their interference was socially permissible. A Westerner in China in the late 1800's, Dr. Arthur Smith, observed the following case of family intervention in support of their daughter:

"....The daughter-in-law had been repeatedly and shamefully abused by the family of her husband, which had been remonstrated with in vain by the family of the girl, the latter family mustered a large force, went to the house of the mother-in-law, destroyed the furniture, beat the other family severely, and dragged the old mother-in-law out into the street, where she was left screaming with what strength remained to her, and covered with blood, in which condition she was seen by foreigners."[2]

The sociologist, C. K. Yang, wrote about another case of clan intervention in a village near Nanjing in the 1940's:

"The wife had one appreciable form of protection against mistreatment from her husband and his family-- her own parents' family and clan. Since marriage was the joint affair of the two families, domestic quarrels between husband and wife might develop into a conflict between the two families. The wife's parents might visit the husband and his family members to demand that they cease the mistreatment or to seek redress for a wrong. If the wife's family was poorer or weaker than the husband's and such action would be ineffective, and the wife's cause was an obviously just one, the wife's clan might intercede and the issue would become a point of contention between the two clans. In the Wong's printed copy of their clan genealogy there was a rule forbidding male clan members from marrying any girl of a Zhen clan in a village about three miles away, the result of a conflict between the two clans caused by the mistreatment of a Wong girl married into the Zhen clan."[3]

Sometimes the daughter-in-law would escape to her natal home and only come back after intervention of a third party or "peace maker." So, a young bride's family could provide a placed to go until tempers cooled and they were often a source of support. Her new family did have some vested interest in her:

--- They had paid money as a bride price for her and would want to receive repayment from her in the form of labor.

--- Their son needed a wife to fulfill duties of marriage and having children, so it was important to have the daughter-in-law stay within the family.

--- Through the marriage of their son to a woman of another clan, the family had made valuable connections that could be called on in time of need.

Therefore, the young bride had some support from her natal family and her husband's family would not wish to lose their investment in her. The woman herself could be her best protection against abuse and ill treatment. A clever young woman could manipulate the joint family situation in several ways:

--- By great discipline she could act the perfect daughter-in-law. Passive and beyond criticism, she could keep her own emotions and thoughts to herself until age and childbirth gave her more status.

--- A young bride might become close to her husband and enlist his support against his mother. Filial duty and the older ties of mother/son probably made this fairly unusual in the early years of marriage.

2. Arthur H. Smith, *Village Life in China* (New York: Fleming H. Revell Company, 1899), p. 277.

3. C. K. Yang, *A Chinese Village in Early Communist Transition* (Cambridge, Mass.: MIT Press, 1959), p. 90.

--- A woman with a powerful personality sometimes chose opposite strategy. She would dominate her new husband and his parents by threats of temper fits and even use physical retaliation. The Chinese woman as "shrew" was a common type in traditional China. One missionary to China in the 1870's described this type of daughter-in-law:

"When [daughters-in-law] wish to gain a point they scold, scream, go into convulsions and are so violent that all become accustomed to yield, for the sake of peace. No one dares arouse the tiger."[4]

--- As a last resort a young woman could threaten to commit suicide-- or actually carry out suicide-- as an extreme and final revenge against her new family. The self-inflicted death of a daughter-in-law was a terrible blow to a family. They lost the bride price and labor of the daughter-in-law. They would have difficulty securing brides for other sons in the family. Most humiliating, they "lost face" with the community.

The following is an example of the consequences of suicide told by the missionary, Arthur Smith. In some cases a "peace-maker" was brought in to negotiate terms between the two families and to settle the dispute brought on by the suicide. Sometimes the young woman's family did get revenge for her mistreatment and death:

[after the suicide, to avoid a lawsuit] *"...the most bitter enemies are often willing enough to put the matter in the hands of 'peace-talkers.' These represent the village of each of the families, and they meet to agree upon the terms of settlement. These terms will depend altogether upon the wealth or otherwise of the family of the mother-in-law. If this family is a rich one, the opposite party always insist upon bleeding it to the utmost practicable extent. Every detail of the funeral is arranged to be as expensive to the family as possible. There must be a cypress-wood coffin, of a specified size and thickness, a certain variety of funeral clothes, often far in excess of what the coffin could by any possibility contain, and some of them made perhaps of silk or satin. A definite amount is required to be spent in hiring Buddhist or Daoist priests, or both, to read masses at the funeral....*

"The wedding outfit of a bride is often very extensive, but in case of her suicide none of it goes back to her family.[5] We have heard from eyewitnesses of many cases in which huge piles of clothing which had been required for the funeral of such a suicide from the family of the mother-in-law, have been burnt in a vast heap at the grave. We know of one instance in which all the wedding outfit, which had been a large one, wardrobes, tables, mirrors, ornaments, etc., was taken out upon the street and destroyed in the presence of the girl's family. The motive to this is of course revenge, but the ultimate effect of such proceedings is to act as an imperfect check upon the behavior of the mother-in-law and her family toward the daughter-in-law, for whom while she lives the laws of the land have no protection.

"When the funeral actually takes place, under conditions such as we have described, there is great danger that despite the exertions of the 'peace-talkers' from both sides, the dispute may break out anew. At sight of the girl's livid face, the result of death by strangulation, it will not be strange if, excited by the spectacle, her family cry out 'Let her be avenged! Let her be avenged!' To

4. *Chinese Recorder*, Vol. V (1874–75), p. 209.

5. In other words, the property remains with the son and mother-in-law.

keep the women of the girl's family quiet at such a time, is beyond the power of any collection of 'peace-talkers,' however numerous and respectable.... The girl's family complain of everything, the coffin, the clothing, the ornaments for the corpse, and all the appointments generally. But they are soothed by the comforting reminder that the dead are dead, and cannot be brought to life, and also that the resources of the family of the mother-in-law have been utterly exhausted, the last acre of land mortgaged to raise money for the funeral, and that they are loaded besides with a millstone of debt...."[6]

Thus, the consequences of a daughter's-in-law suicide were often ruinous to her family by marriage. Enough young women had taken this drastic form of revenge to have the threat of suicide be a powerful protection against severe abuse. A common method of suicide was for the victim to throw herself down the family well. Thus, she not only brought them humiliation by her suicide but poisoned their water supply with her dead body.

The Chinese daughter-in-law did have some recourse against her mother-in-law. She could sometimes call on her own family for help. She used her own personal resources to gain a place in her new home. Under extreme conditions she used the threat of suicide to get relief or ended her misery in a final act of terrible revenge. Ultimately most daughters-in-law improved their status within the family. They accomplished this by becoming mothers, by growing older and, especially, by becoming mothers-in-law themselves.

Points To Consider

1. It appears that the young Chinese daughters-in-law had only two real protections against abuse from their mothers-in-law:

   A. How did her natal clan or family protect her? Why might her new family be interested in keeping good relationships with her natal family?

   B. Her own personality could help her. Explain how she could use complete passivity or submission to get along with her mother-in-law. How could she perhaps protect herself by developing a terrible temper-- becoming a shrew? Which way would you choose in a similar situation? Why? Have you ever used these techniques? When?

2. The ultimate threat by a daughter-in-law was suicide. Why was this an effective weapon against abuse? The desperate nature of this weapon-- self destruction-- tells something of the position of the young daughter-in-law in traditional China. How would you summarize her position, especially until she gave birth to sons?

6. Smith, *Chinese Village*, pp. 278-81.

D. The Adopted Daughter-in-law

Girls were frequently married in their teens. However, child-marriage at eight or ten does not seem to have been common for traditional Chinese girls as it was in India. Chinese families often did have difficulties finding brides for their sons. There were more men than women in the population and some men married more than one woman because of the accepted customs of concubinage and polygyny. Poor families especially had difficulties finding brides for their sons. They had trouble attracting eligible candidates and were hard pressed to save up a bride price. By their teens girls were quite highly prized.

On the other hand, as infants and young children, girls had at best been tolerated. Female infanticide and the selling of female children was common. Especially in times of famine or other crisis selling a girl child was a possible way out of trouble. Many were bought to become prostitutes or to be serving girls. Another common reason for buying a girl was that this was one way of acquiring a bride for a son.

For a rather small fee a family could buy a little girl to be raised as a future daughter-in-law. This type of marriage was variously called: xiao xi, rearing marriage, xi fu or adopting a daughter-in-law. It seems to have been a marriage custom unique to traditional China.

There were several reasons that a family might choose the xiao xi system:

--- The price of buying a small girl child was much less than a bride price.

--- When the couple married, the wedding provided could be much simpler and cheaper. For example, no grand feasts or no sedan chair need be provided.

--- The adopted daughter-in-law served as a household helper to her adopted family before marriage and would continue to do so afterward.

--- The mother-in-law trained and disciplined her future daughter-in-law from childhood so that she was able to mold her as she wished.

Although much of the literature on the Chinese family only briefly mentions this form of marriage, various scholars have estimated that it was quite common in traditional China.[1] Many times a family would sell their own daughters and adopt girls to raise as wives for their sons.

1. For example, see: Fei Xiaotung, *Peasant Life in China* (London: Routledge & Kegan Paul, Ltd., reprinted, 1976), p. 54. Arthur P. Wolf, "Adopt a Daughter-in-law, Marry a Sister: A Chinese Solution to the Problem of the Incest Taboo," *American Anthropologist*, Vol. 70 (1968), pp. 865-866.

One family in Xiajizhou, Taiwan, saved the costs of six dowries and six bride prices by giving away all six of their daughters and adopting in their places six wives for their six sons.[2]

A mother-in-law might arrange for the adoption of her granddaughter-- replacing her with a xi fu-- without even consulting her daughter-in-law. As xiao xi was cheaper and a surer way to get a pliable daughter-in-law, it is perhaps surprising there were not more of these xiao xi marriages. Two major considerations discouraged more families from adopting daughters-in-law:

--- The family lost the advantages of making marriage alliances with a new clan such as being able to call on relatives by marriage for loans or work assistance.

--- A xiao xi form of marriage was considered inferior to a regular marriage between two clans. The family lost prestige by turning to this form of marriage.[3] The family, by choosing this form of marriage, passed up a chance to gain clan and village approval by giving an elaborate, entertaining wedding. If they gave the wedding they were burdened with both the expense of raising the adopted daughter-in-law and giving the wedding.

Whatever the advantages or disadvantages to the families that adopted these little girls, it seems usually to have been an ugly situation for the little adopted daughter-in-law.

The grown daughter-in-law/bride had her own family connections who were interested in her welfare. The adopted daughter-in-law frequently did not even know who her natal family was. Even if she maintained some communications with her natural parents, she grew up knowing that they had given her up for adoption. She probably deeply resented this and could not feel confident of their intervention in case of abuse, with her adopted mother-in-law.[4]

Perhaps the greatest disadvantage for these little girls was that they had been adopted partly as domestic workers. To get a return on the costs

2. *Ibid.*, p. 867.
3. Arthur P. Wolf, "Adopt a Daughter-in-law, Marry a Sister: A Chinese Solution to the Problem of the Incest Taboo," *American Anthropologist*, Vol. 70 (1968), p. 867.
4. *Ibid.*, p. 871.

of raising them, their adopted family expected a great deal of labor from them. On the other hand, there probably was not the feeling of love extended to these adopted daughters that a natural child might expect. In fact, the mother-in-law might be jealous of the future wife of her son and secretly resent her. As this girl would one day be her daughter-in-law, the future mother-in-law would want to train her to be very submissive and obedient as a child. There is much evidence that these little girls were often treated with great severity-- even cruelty. These next excerpts give some idea of the casual cruelty, even torture, used to discipline them. Dr. Ruth Hemenway went to China in the 1920's and worked in a hospital there until 1941. She treated these two cases involving adopted daughters-in-law:

"A woman carried in a six year old girl [who had been] terribly gashed. 'Who did such a thing to this little girl?' I demanded angrily.

"She is my daughter-in-law. I gave her just punishment,' replied the woman aggressively.

"It was common custom for families to take an infant girl to bring up as the future wife of a small son. It was much cheaper than buying a full-grown bride. Also, women liked to discipline and train their future daughters-in-law in their family ways. This woman had slashed the little girl with shears as 'just punishment.'

"We took in the child for treatment and sent for her own mother. 'We want you to see what that cruel woman did to your child,' we told her. She was horrified. Fortunately she had enough money to buy her daughter back: But most little child-wives had no escape.

"...In December 1926, a fifteen year old was brought into the hospital by her mother-in-law. She was a northern child, sold by her parents

during a famine. She had been brought south to Minjing where three months earlier she had been married to the son of her purchaser. Her new husband loved her very much, but it was traditional for sons never to interfere in the relationship between mother and bride. Unfortunately, his mother hated the young girl. When we examined the girl we found that her back was raw with whiplashes, her neck had been burned with a red hot iron, and one hip had been beaten with stones into a discolored mass. We found deep knife wounds here and there on her body.... She had not been allowed food or drink for a number of days and was in a state of shock. The local police would do nothing."[5]

These examples represent extremes of cruelty toward these adopted daughters-in-law in early 20th century China. However, a modern anthropologist, Margery Wolf, found abundant evidence in her studies of rural Taiwan that xi fu or adopting daughters-in-law continues to be a common practice and that they still are often mistreated:

"Taiwanese folktales and proverbs lean heavily for their pathos on the ill treatment of adopted daughters. Everyday expressions comment on an adopted daughter's life: a girl with a sullen expression has a face like a xi fu; a sobbing child cries like a xi fu; a young girl complains that her parents make her work like a xi fu. From the many anecdotes we were told by and about our neighbors, it is clear that the life of an adopted daughter was not a pleasant one a generation or two ago. Even now these girls are not considered the equals of their foster siblings, but a government campaign to alleviate the worst abuses, along with a generally less tolerant attitude toward human suffering, has greatly improved their lot....

5. Ruth V. Hemenway, *A Memoir of Revolutionary China, 1924-1941* (Amherst, MA: University of Massachusetts Press, 1977), pp. 34, 87 and 138-139.

"In modern Taiwan parents have become very self-conscious about their treatment of adopted daughters, but they still make no pretense of an adopted child being the equal of their own children. Adopted daughters, unless they are the only children of their foster parents, are less likely to go on to middle school than their female classmates. A young woman we knew well spoke to us frankly about her status as an adopted daughter. She was the only adopted child of a couple who had three other children, a girl two years her senior and two younger boys. 'I think the reason I was given out as an adopted daughter was because my father died right after I was born. My mother only had two boys and two girls-- she shouldn't have given me away. No one here has treated me really badly, but not particularly well either. When a girl is an adopted daughter, no matter how well she is treated, she is always a little lower than a real daughter....' "[6]

Points To Consider

1. Review the reasons for adopting a daughter-in-law as a baby or young child rather than acquiring a bride for a son through regular betrothal and marriage.

   A. Give several reasons why the mother-in-law often treated these little girls so harshly and expressed dislike or even hatred of them.

   B. Why do you think the xi fu or adopted daughter-in-law often felt more resentment toward her own family than against her adopted family?

   C. Why do you think the community considered these girls inferior? Why do you think there were so many proverbs and sayings about them?

2. Margery and Arthur Wolf are two anthropologists who studied this form of marriage on Taiwan. The Wolfs observed that there was often strong resistance to marriage on the part of the xi fu and the son she was adopted to marry when the time came for their wedding. Unlike regular Chinese brides and grooms, these young people had grown up together and knew each other well. However, it often took the power of their parents to force them to marry each other against their will.

   A. Why do you think that these young people often felt so strongly against marrying each other?

   B. Margery Wolf estimated that over half of the marriages in parts of Taiwan before 1925 were of adopted daughters-in-law.[7] Although this form of marriage is still legal in Taiwan, it is dying out. Why would you think that adopting a daughter-in-law is losing its popularity as a form of marriage?

6. Margery Wolf, *Women and the Family in Rural Taiwan* (Stanford, California: Stanford University Press, 1972), pp. 172-174.

7. *Ibid.*, p. 171.

E. Adult Women As Single Women

1. Widows in Traditional China

Several books dating from early Chinese history outlined ideal female behavior. Women of the court and gentry women were expected to study these "etiquette" books to learn what was considered proper conduct for high class women. *The Records of Virtuous Women of Ancient and Modern Times,* was a huge collection -- four volumes and 313 chapters of ideal females-- who were to be studied by young women as models of expected behavior.[1] Sixteen chapters of the collection were devoted to "the virtue of not marrying again" when a woman was widowed. The following excerpts from *The Records of Virtuous Women* include some of the methods used by these ideal widows to keep from attracting new husbands or having new marriages arranged for them:

"....Ling Nin shaved her head, next cut off her ears, and finally her nose, after which she was presumably safe [from remarriage].

"A youthful widow of sixteen turned from her husband's deathbed to cut off her ear and throw it into his coffin, and she says: 'I have thus comforted the soul of my husband in the shades.'

"When she had performed the funeral rites and buried her husband, she leaped into a neighboring river, and was drowned.

"The lady Feng was the widow of a statesman and prince.... When the prince died, she looked upon herself only as a person not yet dead.... She remained in her home, wearing the coarsest kind of clothing, eating herbs, and having every arrangement of her household severely proper. Her own family seldom saw her face."[2]

Only a few of the widows in *Records of Virtuous Women of Ancient and Modern Times* actually committed suicide as a sign of devotion to their dead husband or to prevent a second marriage. The ideal widow presented in this collection usually refused remarriage, remained chaste and lived a life of devoted service to her children and her husband's family. There were some cases of suicide of widows. Some objected to being

1. *The Records of Virtuous Women of Ancient and Modern Times* was attributed to Liu Xiang who lived during the Han Dynasty. It was added to during the Ming Dynasty. See editor's preface, A. C. Safford, *Typical Women of China* (London: Kelly Walsh Ltd., 1899), pp. 57–58, 154, 157.
2. *Ibid.*, pp. 57–58, 154, 157.

A memorial arch could be one that was to commemorate chaste widows.

forced by their husband's family to remarry; some did not want to continue living with their husband's family; and some committed suicide as a sign of grief and devotion to their husband's memory. A missionary, Justus Doolittle, reported several of these public suicides in the mid-1800's near the town of Fuzhan. He observed a case of a woman who hanged herself in public with her family and village watching. Another young girl of fourteen, who was only betrothed and not yet married, also committed suicide by public hanging at her fiance's death.[3] These widows had their names recorded on a large tablet. Chaste widows were honored by having ornamental arches raised in recognition of their virtue.

Although the ideal was for a widow never to remarry, many women did marry a second time. Below is a list of items relating to widows and widowers in traditional China.

1. Upon marriage a woman became a permanent part of her husband's family-- they claimed her labor; any children she had belonged to them.

2. *"A test of the married woman's absorption [and acceptance] into her husband's group was her fate on widowhood."[4]*

3. The family of her husband could arrange a marriage for the widow against her will.

4. A widow had no claim on her children. If she remarried and moved away from her first husband's home they remained there-- sometimes she was allowed to take her daughters.

5. A widow could not inherit money, land or goods from her husband.

6. A woman was dishonored if she remarried. On the other hand, widowers were encouraged to remarry. Especially if there were no children from the first marriage, it was considered his duty to provide heirs by remarrying.

7. No sedan chair or elaborate wedding was provided a widow if she remarried.

8. The bride price was much less for a widow than for a bride marrying for the first time.

9. It was harder for a man who was a widower to find a bride than a man who had never been married.

10. Between the ages of 20-50, there were more adult men than women.

11. There were no government laws in traditional China that prevented widows from remarrying.

12. A widow who did not remarry could become head of the household while her sons were children if no other appropriate male was available.

13. Although a widowed mother was supposed to obey an adult son, usually she continued to order his life. Adult sons had been trained in the ideal of filial piety, absolutely to respect their mother's wishes.

14. Mourning customs on death of a spouse from the Jiangzi Valley village of Gaixiangong in the 1930's:[5]

	Period of Mourning	Act of Mourning
Wife	Indefinitely, until the marriage of her son.	Coarse hempen skirt and shoes, white cord on the hair at the beginning then changing to white skirt and shoes, wearing no silk.
Husband	Indefinite, a few months.	Blue button on the hat.

3. Justus Doolittle, *Social Life of the Chinese* (London: Sampson Low, Son and Marston, 1868), pp. 77-79.
4. Maurice Freedman, *Lineage Organization in Southeastern China* (London: The Athlone Press, 1958), p. 31.
5. Fei Xiantong, *Peasant Life in China* (London: Routledge & Kegan Paul, Ltd., 1962), p. 78.

100   **Nineteenth century widow.**

15. An unmarried man was in a very difficult position as women did a great deal of domestic work; he needed to continue the family line by having sons and it was dishonorable not to remarry.

16. The emperors granted chaste or virtuous widows (including those that committed suicide) the honor of putting their names on a monument or stone arch. Small pensions were also granted to poor and worthy widows.

Group Exercise

1. List specific items relating to widows and widowers that might discourage widow remarriage in traditional China. Give brief reasons for your choice.

2. Which items would seem to encourage widow remarriage? Why?

3. Why do you think older widows might choose not to remarry, while younger women usually did?

4. Would a widower be encouraged to remarry? Why or why not?

E. 2. Divorce in Traditional China

According to tradition Confucius laid down seven reasons for which a man could "put away" (divorce) his wife. These grounds were a part of the legal code of the empire until the fall of the Manchu Dynasty and final revision of the codes.

The seven grounds on which the husband could divorce his wife:

1. She is rebellious or unfilial toward her parents-in-law.

2. She has failed to produce a son.

3. She has been unfaithful to her husband.

4. She has shown jealousy toward her husband's other women.

5. She has a repulsive and incurable disease (such as leprosy).

6. She is given to hurtful talk, talebearing and talking too much.

7. She is a thief.[1]

The three grounds on which a wife can prevent her husband from putting her away (divorcing her):

1. She has mourned three years for her husband's parents.

2. She has no family to which to return.

3. She married her husband when he was poor, and now he is rich.

The grounds on which a wife can put away (divorce) her husband:

   None

In reality, there was almost no divorce in traditional China:

--- Women could not divorce their husbands.

--- Men from the gentry class did not need to divorce their wives.

--- Peasant men could not afford to divorce their wives.

The Woman and Divorce
When a Chinese woman married she acquired a real family for the first time. She had had no permanent status in her natal home. Her family by marriage was to be hers for life. At her death it was on her husband's ancestoral tablet that her name would be enscribed. If she left this home she left what little property she owned and she had no custody rights for her children. They remained with their father.

If a wife was very unhappy, she might separate from her husband and go home to her own parents. "Peacemakers" would usually patch up the husband/wife dispute and she would go back to her husband. There was strong social pressure for her to return, but if she refused she could be abducted by her husband's family and legally compelled to return. Often her fear for the mistreatment of her children or the threat of her husband's

---

1. This appears to have been made a ground for divorce to prevent young wives who had come from poor families to wealthier ones from sending money or goods home to help their parents.

taking a second wife would compel her to go back. Many of these unhappy marriages in traditional China involved a series of separations with renewed attempts at husband/wife reconciliations.[2]

The Gentry Man and Divorce

The husband of the gentry class had the duties of caring for his wife and assuring her pregnancies so that the family line of sons could be carried on, but otherwise he was free to:

--- live in separate quarters

--- take a concubine or concubines

--- see his wife only for household discussions and, until she was about forty years old, maintain occasional sexual contact with her

If a gentry husband was not getting along with his wife or if she was barren, he did not need to divorce her. Divorce was not socially approved. Therefore, the man of the gentry class merely separated himself from his wife while remaining officially married or took a concubine to be assured of children.

Peasant Men and Divorce

A wife was essential to a peasant man. She provided domestic labor while he farmed and, depending on the area of China, also contributed to the farm labor force at the peak work period. She might also bring in extra money through various kinds of home industries such as silk manufacture. She was the means of continuing the family line through giving birth to children. His status rose within the joint family and community with his marriage. Before marriage-- no matter how old he was-- he was considered to be a "boy"; afterward he became a "man."

Also, the peasant wife had either cost the family a bride price or, if she was an adopted daughter-in-law, the cost of raising her. The family was anxious

not to lose this investment by a divorce. Since the emphasis was on the bride's worth to the family, little consideration was given to whether the husband and wife were all that happy together. In fact, the occasional divorce that did occur often seems to have been instigated by the husband's mother who hated her daughter-in-law rather than by the husband.

Divorce, then, was a rare occurrence in traditional China. If a marriage situation were unbearable for a woman, her bleak choices were temporary separations from her husband or suicide. If the marriage were unbearable for a gentry man, he kept to separate quarters and took a concubine. If the marriage were unbearable for a peasant man it appears that he might have reacted with violence against his wife or he might have become submissive and passive in response to his wife's temper-- avoiding her as much as was possible.

Points To Consider

1. What things do you notice about the grounds on which a man could divorce his wife? What do these grounds show about the way the ideal woman was expected to behave in traditional China?

2. What things do you notice about the grounds on which a woman could prevent a divorce? Why do you think each one gave a woman the right to demand that she not be divorced?

3. Even though it was possible for a husband to get a divorce from his wife on seven grounds, there was almost no divorce in traditional China. List some reasons why this was the case.

2. C. K. Yang, *The Chinese Family in the Communist Revolution* (Cambridge, MA: MIT Press, 1959), pp. 64-65.

4. A well-documented type of Chinese woman was the "Village Shrew." She used her tongue as an effective weapon to get her way with her husband, his family, or with neighbors. R. F. Johnston, a British official in Weihaiwei, around the turn of the century, described this type of female tyrant:

"Women, indeed, are at the root of a large proportion of the cases heard in the courts. No insignificant part of the duty of a magistrate in Weihaiwei consists in the taming of village shrews. The number of such women in China is much larger than might be supposed by many Europeans, who regard the average Chinese wife as the patient slave of a tyrannical master....

"The abject terror with which an uncompromising village shrew is regarded by her male relatives and by neighbors frequently creates situations which would be somewhat funny, if they did not contain an element of sadness....

"The northern Chinese use a curious and highly appropriate expression to describe a woman of the shrew type. They call her a ma-jie-di or 'Curse-the-street woman.' This is the kind of female who by blows or threats drives her husband out of the house, follows him into the road, and there-- if he has sought safety in flight-- proceeds to pour torrents of abuse at the top of her voice upon her male and female neighbors and all and sundry passers-by. If the village street happens to be entirely empty she will address her remarks to the papered windows, on the chance of there being listeners behind them. As a rule the neighbors will come out to 'see the fun.' The abused persons generally refrain from answering back and the men-- taking care to keep out of reach of the nails of the ma-jie-di-- gaze at her thoughtfully and with impassive features until her spent voice fades into a hoarse whisper or physical exhaustion lays her helpless on the ground."[3]

Why did the following aspects of traditional Chinese culture perhaps encourage peasant women to become "curse-the-street women?"

A. The powerless position and low status of young women as wives/ daughters-in-law.

B. The importance of men keeping "face"-- not bringing discredit on themselves that would reflect on the family.

C. The fact that peasant men usually could not afford concubines. The fact that there were grounds on which a man could divorce his wife, but men rarely did so.

3. R. F. Johnson, *Lion and Dragon in Northern China* (New York: E. P. Dutton and Company, 1910), pp. 197, 198, 201-202.

F. The Custom of Footbinding

One of the most noticed customs to do with women of any world cultural area was the traditional Chinese practice of "footbinding." When a Chinese girl was six or seven years old the process was started. A long narrow bandage was wrapped tightly around each foot so as to force the toes under against the sole. The large toe was left unbound, but the bandaging was so tightly done against the heel of the foot that the toes were eventually pulled back against the heel.[1] If the bandages were applied skillfully, after several years the ideal of a three-or-four-inch "lotus" (the Chinese expression for the tiny foot) might be achieved. The next pages show a photograph of bound feet, the eventual physical results of the binding process as seen in the X-rays and some drawings of the tiny shoes worn.

In an earlier section, the beginning of this process was described by a missionary observer. In this next excerpt a young Chinese girl tells what it was like to have her feet bound:

"Born into an old-fashioned family at Pingxi, I was inflicted with the pain of footbinding when I was seven years old. I was an active child who liked to jump about, but from then on my free and optimistic nature vanished.... It was the first lunar month of my seventh year that my ears were pierced and fitted with gold earrings. I was told that a girl had to suffer twice, through ear piercing and footbinding. Binding started in the second lunar month; mother consulted references in order to select a lucky day for it. I wept and hid in a neighbor's home, but mother found me, scolded me, and dragged me home. She shut the bedroom door, boiled water, and from a box withdrew binding, shoes, knife, needle, and thread. I begged for a one-day postponement, but mother refused: 'Today is a lucky day,' she said. 'If bound today, your feet will never hurt; if bound tomorrow, they will.' She washed and placed powder on my feet and cut the toenails. She then bent my toes toward the sole with a binding cloth ten feet long and two inches wide doing the right foot first and then the left. She finished binding and ordered me to walk, but when I did the pain proved unbearable.

"That night, mother wouldn't let me remove the shoes. My feet felt on fire and I couldn't sleep; mother struck me for crying. On the following days, I tried to hide but was forced to walk on my feet. Mother hit me on my hands and feet for resisting. Beatings and curses were my lot for secretly loosening the wrappings. The feet were washed and rebound after three or four days....

After several months, all toes but the big one were pressed against the inner surface. Whenever I ate fish or freshly killed meat, my feet would swell, and the pus would drip. Mother criticized me for placing pressure on the heel in walking, saying that my feet would never assume a pretty shape. Mother would remove the

1. Howard Levy, *Chinese Footbinding* (New York: Walton Rawls, 1966), pp. 23–24.

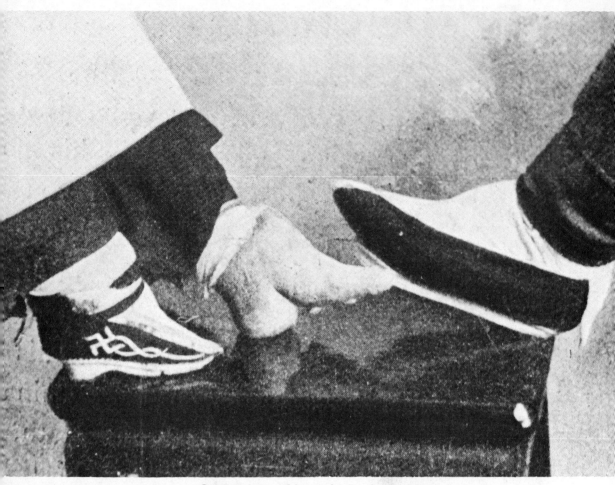

Comparison of bound to unbound feet

bindings and wipe the blood and pus which dripped from my feet. She told me that only with removal of the flesh could my feet become slender. If I mistakenly punctured a sore, the blood gushed like a stream. My somewhat fleshy big toes were bound with small pieces of cloth and forced upwards, to assume a new moon shape.

"Every two weeks, I changed to new shoes. Each new pair was one to two tenths of an inch smaller than the previous one. The shoes were unyielding, and it took pressure to get into them. Though I wanted to sit passively by the kang [stove], Mother forced me to move around. After changing more than ten pairs of shoes, my feet were reduced to a little over four inches. I had been binding for a month when my younger sister started; when no one was around, we would weep together. In summer, my feet smelled offensively because of pus and blood; in winter, my feet felt cold because of lack of circulation and hurt if they got too near the kang and were struck by warm air

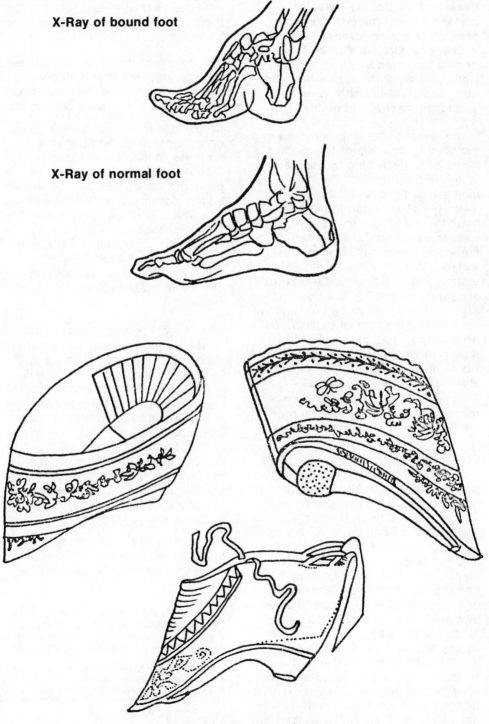

X-Ray of bound foot

X-Ray of normal foot

Drawings of tiny shoes

currents. Four of the toes were curled in like so many dead caterpillars; no outsider would ever have believed that they belonged to a human being. It took two years to achieve the three-inch model. My toenails pressed against the flesh like thin paper. The heavily-creased sole couldn't be scratched when it itched or soothed when it ached. My shanks were thin, my feet became humped, ugly, and smelled badly; how I envied the natural-footed!"[2]

In this description of the process of footbinding, the role of the mother is particularly disturbing to people today. In traditional China it was the mothers and grandmothers who insisted that their daughters have bound feet and saw to it that they were properly bound at an early age. For women who had themselves suffered through the process of footbinding their insistence that their daughters also suffer is a perplexing aspect of this custom. Not all mothers were as harsh as the one described here. Some could barely stand to watch their daughter's suffering and would hire someone to carry out the binding. But many traditional Chinese women-- rich and poor-- had bound feet and the women of the family carried on this tradition.

Fortunately, the suffering described here did not continue. After about two years the bound feet lost all feeling-- becoming completely numb. Then the feet only hurt when they were unbound and circulation was restored. However, having tiny feet affected these Chinese women in many ways. Their walk became permanently changed. *"They sway, or rather, wobble from side to side with stiff knees, as though on stilts, for the whole weight of the body is balanced on the point of the heel and the ball of the great toe."[3]* Because of their tiny feet, their pace became painfully slow and their mobility limited.[4] If the binding had been severely tight, these women

often had to use a cane to walk or even be carried. The tiny feet of traditional Chinese women became a symbol of their status. But footbinding was also a real way to limit their activities and to restrict them to narrow, secluded lives close to home.

The origins of this custom in Chinese history are somewhat a matter of speculation. Various theories about how it came about have been given:

In Chinese folklore a fox fairy took on a human form and became an empress of the Shang Dynasty (1500-1000 B.C.). However, her fox paws did not change to human feet so she covered them with bandages to conceal her true identity as a fox fairy. Because she was the empress, all the women began to imitate her and tightly bandaged their feet. In this way the custom of footbinding came into practice in very ancient times.[5]

More scholarly explanations rule out footbinding until a much later period, probably at the end of the Tang Dynasty (600-900 A.D.). There is much evidence in art and literature that women in the Tang period lived active lives and did not bind their feet. Zhang Bangji, a Chinese writer of the 12th century A.D. (Song Dynasty), described the origin of footbinding in the following way: He claimed that footbinding had begun at the end of the Tang Dynasty by an emperor-poet called Li Yu.

"According to the reference, Li Yu had a favored palace concubine named Lovely Maiden who was a

2. Quoted in Levy, *Footbinding*, pp. 26-28 from a Chinese collection of descriptions of footbinding.

3. Hermann H. Ploss, Max and Paul Bartels, *Woman* (London: Wilham Heinemann, Ltd., 1935), Vol. I, p. 268.

4. Section III-A-3 described a Chinese grandmother with bound feet who had walked for three days to get to a medical clinic. The doctors were amazed at her journey not so much because of her age but because she had managed it with bound feet.

5. Levy, *Footbinding*, p. 37.

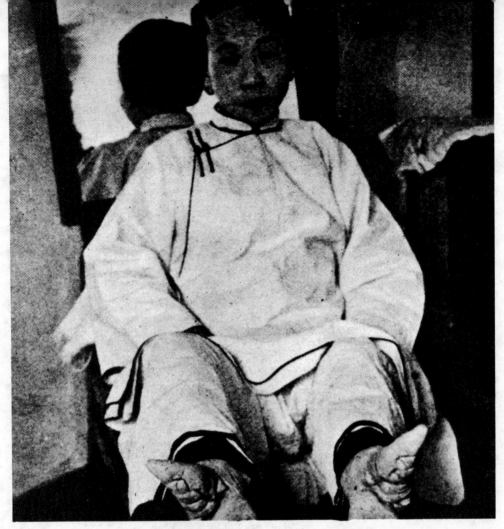

Gentry woman with unwrapped tiny "lotus" feet

slender-waisted beauty and a gifted dancer. He had a six foot high lotus constructed for her out of gold; it was decorated lavishly with pearls.... Lovely Maiden was ordered to bind her feet with white silk cloth to make the tips look like the points of a moon sickle. She then danced in the center of the lotus, whirling about like a rising cloud." [6]

There are other, later references that seem to associate bound feet with dancing. The original footbinding may have been meant to accomplish what western toe shoes do for ballet dancers-- permitting dancing on a pointed toe. If this was the origin of footbinding the original purpose was so completely lost that later women

with bound feet could hardly walk, much less dance.[7] It appears most likely that footbinding began at the palace level and filtered down to the lower classes becoming quite general by the end of the Song Dynasty in the 13th century.

The binding of Chinese women's feet was but one aspect of their loss of status during the period from about 900 to 1300 A.D. During this time women's intellectual activities were restricted, it became customary for widows not to remarry and seclusion

6. Quoted in Levy, *Footbinding*, p. 39.
7. *Ibid.*, pp. 40-41.

Bathing of tiny lotus feet-- shoe and bindings have been removed from the foot to the right.

of women at home became an ideal. Unfortunately, because footbinding started with the upper classes, it came to be considered low class to have big feet. Smaller and smaller feet came to be the ideal until the deformed, tiny lotus foot was considered to be the height of sensual beauty. Upper class mothers feared that their daughters would not find suitable husbands if they did not have properly bound feet. Low class parents hoped that if they tightly bound their daughters' feet to achieve the three-inch ideal, their daughters might marry into a higher class or more wealth. Mothers forced their daughters to have bound feet, as this made them more likely to have marriage choices and future security. Much poetry and many love stories were devoted to glorifying tiny, bound feet. The notion that big feet were ugly and low class and small feet beautiful became cultural standards, making it very difficult to get rid of this custom.

The following excerpt is about a Chinese girl whose association with anti-footbinding Christian missionaries in the early part of the 20th century makes it possible for her to try to break away from her mother's insistence that she bind her feet:

"When I was twelve I entered the [missionary] school. About the school door, I saw many happy girls, playing games and skipping, and I thought I was in Heaven. The

happiness and hope in my heart could not be expressed. But there was one thing which troubled me deeply. My feet were still tightly bound. I could have taken the bandages off; but Mother had laid down the rule that if I did not keep my feet bound, I could not go to school. There were other small-foot girls like me, and they felt as I did. Some of the older pupils who had natural feet,...brought scissors and wanted to cut our foot bandages. They looked every day to see if our feet were still bound. At first I was willing to endure the pain for the privilege of coming to school. Then, when I saw the big feet of the others and looked down at my own three-inch 'golden lotuses,' I thought mine were too disgraceful and too ugly for words. So I ceased to care and took off my bandages. And when it rained, I took off my shoes too and waded in the pools in the courtyard like my big-foot schoolmates....

"Mother saw that my small feet were getting big again, and was very angry and hurt. She scolded me for disobeying her, and at the same time said that the school authorities took too little thought of the face of the parents. It was true, of course, that in her eyes a pair of fanlike big feet were a great disgrace. How could she be satisfied with five-inch feet, as the result of all the trouble she had taken to make them small?" [8]

Points To Consider

1. What explanations have there been for the origin of footbinding? By most estimates this custom began around 900 or 1000 A.D. — it only went out of fashion in the 1920's and there are still older women in China with bound feet. Why do you think that Chinese women continued to bind their feet for about 1000 years? Why do you think the custom was so hard to get rid of?

2. In what economic class did this custom begin? Why did other classes of women accept this strange custom? What effects might footbinding have on families that needed women's labor?

3. Do you think that the custom of footbinding would have been so widespread if traditional Chinese women had had higher status? In what specific ways was footbinding a sign of their low status?

4. Why do you think it is the mother who is disturbed when her daughter unbinds her feet in the last story? What encourages the young woman to unbind her feet against her mother's orders?

The custom of footbinding became a major target for reformers in China. To many people footbinding seemed both to restrict women's physical activities and to symbolize their subordinate status. However, historical China had many traditions that applied to women. Women of China had held power as Empress Dowagers. Women warriors had fought in wars, rebellions and, even as bandits. Women had become religious nuns, artists and poets. Although women were restricted by the Confucian system, it also provided the promise of high status in old age. The richness of China's cultural traditions has meant increasing opportunities of women.

In *Women in Modern China* some aspects of these topics are discussed:
• The diversity of traditions for women which have been present in China's minority groups.
• Various individuals and groups who have worked for reform for women — through slow change in China or by revolutionary activities.
• The Communist Revolution's effect on women's lives.
• Some suggestions about the current status of Chinese women from travelers' accounts, statistics and reports from China.

8. Xie Bingying, *Girl Rebel* (New York: John Day, 1940), pp. 32-33, 37.

Selected Bibliography

NON-FICTION

Belden, Jack. *China Shakes the World.* New York: Harper Bros., 1949.

Bullough, Vern L. *The Subordinate Sex.* New York: Penguin Books, 1974.

Croll, Elisabeth. *Feminism and Socialism in China.* London: Routledge & Kegan Paul, 1978.

———————————— *The Women's Movement in China.* London: Russell Press, 1974.

———————————— *Women in Rural Development: The People's Republic of China.* Geneva: International Labour Office, 1979.

Crook, Isabel and David. *Revolution in a Chinese Village: Ten Mile Inn.* London: Routledge and Kegan Paul, 1959.

Curtin, Katie. *Women in China.* New York: Pathfinder Press, 1975.

Davin, Delia. *Woman-Work: Women and the Party in Revolutionary China.* Oxford: Clarendon Press, 1976.

Goode, William J. *World Revolution and Family Patterns.* New York: The Free Press, 1963.

Hemenway, Ruth. *A Memoir of Revolutionary China, 1924-1941.* Amherst: University of Massachusetts Press, 1977.

Hinton, William. *Fanshen.* New York: Monthly Review Press, 1966.

Horn, Dr. Joshua. *Away with All Pests.* New York: Monthly Review Press, 1969.

Lang, Olga. *Chinese Family and Society.* New Haven: Archon Books, 1968.

Levy, Marion J. *The Family Revolution in Modern China.* New York: Atheneum, 1968.

Lin, Yao-hua. *The Golden Wing: A Sociological Study of Chinese Families.* New York: Oxford University Press, 1948.

Mace, David and Vera. *Marriage: East and West.* New York: Dolphin Books, 1959.

Myrdal, Jan. *Report from a Chinese Village.* New York: Random House, 1966.

Myrdal, Jan and Gun Kessle. *China: The Revolution Continued.* New York: Pantheon Books, 1971.

New Women in New China. Peking: Foreign Language Press, 1972.

Sidel, Ruth. *Women and Child Care in China.* New York: Penguin Books, 1972.

Smedley, Agnes. *Chinese Destinies.* New York: The Vanguard Press, 1922.

———————————— *Portraits of Chinese Women in Revolution.* New York: The Feminist Press, 1976.

Snow, Helen Foster. *Women in Modern China.* The Hague: Mouton & Co., 1967.

Waln, Nora. *The House of Exile.* Boston: Little, Brown and Co., 1933.

Winnington, Alan. *Tibet: Record of a Journey.* London: Lawrence & Wishart Ltd., 1957.

Wolf, Margery. "Chinese Women: Old Skills in a New Context," in Michelle Zimbalist Rosaldo and Louise Lamphere, eds., *Women, Culture, and Society.* Stanford: Stanford University Press, 1974.

_____ *The House of Lin.* Englewood Cliff: Prentice Hall, 1968.

Wolf, Margery and Roxanne Witke. *Women in Chinese Society.* Stanford: Stanford University Press, 1975.

Yang, Qingkun (Ch'ing-k'un). *Chinese Communist Society: The Family and the Village.* Cambridge: M.I.T. Press, 1959.

Yang, Martin C. *A Chinese Village: Taiton, Shantung Province.* New York: Columbia University Press, 1945.

Young, Marilyn ed., *Women in China: Studies in Social Change and Feminism.* Ann Arbor: University of Michigan Press, 1973.

BIOGRAPHY

Ayscough, Florence. *Chinese Women: Yesterday and Today.* Boston: Houghton Mifflin, 1937.

(Chao, Buwei) Zhao Buwei. *Autobiography of a Chinese Woman.* New York: John Day, 1947.

(Chow Chung-Cheng) Zhou Zhungzheng. *The Lotus Pool.* New York: Appleton-Century-Crofts, 1961.

DerLing, Princess. *Kowtow.* New York: Dodd, Mead & Co., 1929.

Hahn, Emily. *The (Soong) Song Sisters.* Garden City: Garden City Publishing Co., 1945.

Han Suyin. *Birdless Summer.* New York: G. P. Putnams, 1968.

_____ . *The Crippled Tree.* New York: G. P. Putnams, 1965.

_____ . *A Mortal Flower.* New York: G. P. Putnams, 1965.

Hibbert, Eloise Talcott. *Embroidered Gauze: Portraits of Famous Chinese Ladies.* London: John Lane, 1938.

Liang Yan (Briggs, Margaret). *Daughter of the Khans.* New York: W. W. Norton Company, 1955.

Pruitt, Ida. *A Daughter of Han.* Stanford: Stanford University Press, 1967.

Wales, Nym (Helen Snow). *The Chinese Communists: Sketches and Autobiographies of the Old Guard.* Westport: Greenwood Publishing, 1972.

Witke, Roxanne. *Comrade Chiang Ch'ing.* Boston: Little Brown & Co., 1977.

Wong Su-ling and Earl Herbert Cressy. *Daughter of Confucius.* New York: Farrar, Straus & Young, 1952.

LITERATURE

Buck, Pearl. *The Mother.* New York: John Day, 1934.

Chen (Jo-Hsi) Rouxi. *The Execution of Mayor Yin and Other Stories from the Great Proletarian Cultural Revolution.* Bloomington: Indiana University Press, 1978.

(Ho) He Jingzhi and (Ting) Ding Yi. *The White-haired Girl, An Opera in Five Acts.* Peking: Foreign Languages Press, 1954.

(Pa Chin) Ba Jin. *Family.* New York: Anchor Books, 1972.

Rexroth, Kenneth and Ling Zhung. *The Orchid Boat: Women Poets of China.* New York: McGraw Hill, 1972.

Seeds and Other Stories. Peking: Foreign Languages Press, 1972.

(Tsao Hsueh-Chin) Zao Xuejin. *Dream of the Red Chamber.* New York: Doubleday Anchor, 1958.

Glossary

Anthropology: (Anthropologist) The branch of social science that deals with cultural development and social customs of people. Often anthropologists study small groups of people to observe their social organizations.

Archaeology: (Archaeological) The science of studying prehistoric or historic peoples by analyzing their artifacts and other remains. Often involves excavation or digging up these remains at the site of an ancient society.

Artifacts: Any object made or shaped by humans.

Autopsy: Dissection and study of a body after death to determine such things as the state of health of the person upon death or the cause of death.

Boxer Rebellion: A rebellion led against Westerners in 1899–1900 that was secretly encouraged by the empress dowager Ci Xi . Foreign troops defeated the rebels and subjected China to many economic demands.

Bride Price: Money or goods paid to the bride's family by the groom's family.

CCP: Chinese Communist Party, members of which follow Marxist-Leninist ideas of socialist government.

Cadre: Various types of Communist Party and government workers at all levels.

Cash or String of Cash: A string of small coins strung together through a hole in the center of each coin-- worth a few pennies.

Chaste: (Chastity) Pure; not having had sexual intercourse outside of marriage.

Concubine: (Concubinage) A secondary wife who has some of the rights and privileges of a wife, but has less status than a regular wife.

Confucius: (Confucian principles or philosophy) A Chinese scholar and teacher (c. 551–497 B.C.). Though his life is surrounded by legend, the sayings and writings attributed to him form the basis of traditional Chinese social philosophy.

Courtesan: A prostitute who associates with men of power or wealth. Often known for their beauty and intelligence.

Cultural Revolution: A campaign (1965–67) that Mao and the Red Guards led against his "enemies." The term generally refers to the period in which intellectuals were under suspicion and in which Jiang Qing (Mao's wife) came to have more power.

Daoism:	A Chinese philosophy or religion attributed to the probably legendary figure Lao-tzu who was supposed to have lived around the 6th century B.C. Started with the idea of attaining happiness by living a simple, natural life. In later Chinese history, Daoism became mixed with magic and superstition.
Dowry:	Money or goods paid to the groom's family by the bride's family.
Empress Dowager:	The widow of the emperor, who often was powerful in China as the regent for her son or foster son.
Eunuch:	Man who was castrated so that he would not pose a sexual threat.
Filial Piety:	A Confucian idea that sons and daughters owe absolute obedience to their parents (or in the case of a daughter-in-law, to her parents-in-law).
Gentry:	A class of well-off landowners of traditional China. They did not have titles as nobles, but were considered wellbred.
Guan Yin:	(Kwan-Yin, Kwanyin) The Buddhist female god of mercy in China who was prayed to particularly by women and sailors.
Guomindang:	A political party organized in China in 1912. It was originally a coalition of various groups who wanted a Chinese republic, not war-lord rule. In 1927, however, Chiang Kai-shek took control of the Guomindang part and led it until his death. After the defeat of the Guomindang by the Chinese Communists, the Party moved to Taiwan and ruled there. The Party was also known as the "Nationalist" Party.
Hundred Flowers Campaign:	A campaign started by Mao to open up the Communist Party to more criticism. When the criticisms became threatening to the bureaucracy, however, Mao closed off the speeches. Ding Ling was purged as a result of her comments in the campaign.
Infanticide:	(in-*fan*-ti-cide) The killing of infants.
Jade:	A semi-valuable, usually green, stone highly valued in China and used for jewelry and carvings.
Joint Family:	Practice whereby a group of people with a common male ancestor live together, share common economic resources, tasks and living space.
Kang:	Heated brick bed often part of a Chinese peasant home.
Kou tou or (Kowtow):	A Chinese custom of kneeling and then touching the forehead to the ground as an act of reverence or apology.
Long March:	Chinese Communists retreated from Chiang Kai-shek's army, moving from Kiangsi to Yenan in October, 1934 to October, 1936.
Manchu:	The name of a group of Northern invaders who conquered China and ruled it from 1644-1912 A.D.

Mongols: A group of Northwestern invaders of China who ruled China from 1279–1368 A.D. Inner Mongolia is not an "autonomous" region of China.

Matriarchy: (matriarchal) Where the mother is head of the household and descent lines are traced through the mother.

May Fourth Movement: A Chinese nationalistic movement that began with protests against the Allied powers after the Versailles Treaty gave Japan rights to Chinese territory. The height of the demonstrations were May 4, 1919, but the movement itself encouraged more questioning in not only politics, but also arts and social customs.

Natal Family: Family into which a person is born.

Nationalist Party: Another name for Guomindang forces led by Chiang Kai-shek who opposed the Chinese Communists.

New Life Movement: Chiang Kai-shek's program of reform in China that generally went back to Confucian ideas concerning women's household roles.

Norsu: A small tribal group located in the rugged Cool Mountains of southwestern China. Commonly called "lolos" (a derogatory term) by the Han Chinese, these slavers were feared by local peoples until the CCP persuaded them to give up their slaves.

Nun: A woman who is a part of a religious order and often lives in a nunnery or convent. Usually they are not married and often live a life devoted entirely to their religion.

Patriarchy: (patriarchal) Where the father is head of the household and descent lines are traced through the father.

Politburo: Ruling body of the CCP (Chinese Communist Party).

Polyandry: The practice of a woman having more than one husband at a time.

Polygamy: The practice of having several spouses at the same time.

Polygyny: The practice of a man having more than one wife at one time.

Pre-historic: History of people before recorded events and known mainly through archaeological discoveries.

Purged: Eliminated from all Party power positions and usually condemned as a traitor to Communism. Though not always jailed or physically harmed, a person who has been purged is often treated as an outcast.

Red Lantern: Women's divisions involved in the Boxer Rebellion.

Shrew: A woman with a violent temper and often having loud speech or temper outbursts.

Sibling: A brother or sister.

Taiping Rebellion:	A rebellion against the Manchu government in 1848–65. Women served in the armies of the Taiping, but in separate regiments. The rebellion was put down with the aid of Western troops.
Tantric Cult:	A part of Hinduism (a religion of India) that stressed women's importance and the power of the female god, Shakti.
Uxorilocal:	Husband comes to live with the wife's family.
War Lords:	Military dictators who, using private armies, gained control of parts of China in the period before World War II.
Wet Nurse:	A woman who nurses another woman's baby.
White Lotus Rebellion:	An uprising against the Manchu government in the 1780's, women fought with men. The rebellion was unsuccessful, but may have been a pattern for later rebellions.
White Terror:	A term which applies to Chiang Kai-shek's attempt at eliminating the Communists in China in 1927. Communist-- or even bobbed-haired-- women were particular targets for attack.
Yin and Yang:	A Chinese philosophy (a part of both Confucianism and Daoism) that there are two principles (Yin=negative, dark and feminine and Yang=positive, bright and masculine). These two principles influence the destinies of all creatures.

Explanation of Pinyin

The following is a reprinted explanation of the *pinyin* system of Romanization taken from: Molly Coye and Jon Livingston, *China Yesterday and Today*. New York: Bantam Books, 1979. pp. 360-362.

For one hundred years, since the time of the Western missionaries' first intrusion into China, Europeans and Americans have used a variety of conflicting and confusing methods to represent Chinese sounds. By now one set, the Wade-Giles system, has come to be used fairly regularly by American and British scholars, but it gives misleading and undependable indications of the true Chinese sounds. Twenty years ago the Chinese developed -- and in 1979 put into formal use -- a perfectly adequate system called *pinyin*.

The system is very simple. All vowel sounds are pronounced "pure," as they are in Latin. For instance, *ao* is pronounced to rhyme with "cow," *ai* to rhyme with "high," *ou* to rhyme with "throw."

On the following page is the official phonetic alphabet table published in Peking from *The Beijing Review*, No. 1, 1979.

A bit of further explanation is helpful toward understanding several sets of consonants for which we have only a single spelling and sound in English. For these the Chinese have two pronunciations and have thus chosen to use some English letters in unusual ways, as outlined below. We include these here in addition to the official chart because they are the most troublesome for English speakers. The letters *c, z, x,* and *q,* when used for Chinese, do not correspond to common English sounds, whereas the others in the table generally do.

Pinyin	English	Similar English Sound
x	sh	*sheet* (tongue lies flat)
sh	sh	*shock* (tongue touches roof of mouth)
j	j	*jeep* (*y* sound after j; tongue lies flat)

Pinyin	Wade–Giles	As in ...
a	a	far
b	p	be
c	ts'	its
ch	ch'	church[1]
d	t	do
e	e	*e* in her
ei	ei	way
f	f	foot
g	k	go
h	h	her[1]
i	i	eat; sir[2]
ie	ieh	yes
j	ch	jeep
k	k'	kind[1]
l	l	land
m	m	me
n	n	no
o	o	law
p	p'	par[1]
q	ch'	cheek
r	j	*z* in azure[3]
s	s, ss, sz	sister
sh	sh	shore
t	t'	top[1]
u	u	too[4]
v	v	*
w	w	want
x	hs	she
y	y	yet
z	ts, tz	zero
zh	ch	*j* in jump

Pinyin	English	Similar English Sound
zh	j	*j*aunt (no *y* sound; tongue points up)
ch	ch	*ch*unk (no *y* sound; tongue points up)
q	ch	*ch*ew (*y* sound after *ch*)

1. Strongly aspirated.
2. In syllables beginning with *c, ch, r, s, sh, z, zh*.
3. Or pronounced like English *r* but not rolled.
4. Or as in French *tu* or German *Munchen*.
* Used only in foreign and national minority words, and local dialects.

Three other letters vary from English; *z* is harder than English *z* and is closer to *ds* in "ads." *c* is equivalent to *ts* in "hats." The Chinese *r* is not quite comparable to the French *z*, as claimed; rather it is closer to the combination *r + zh* sound in Czech represented by *r*, as in the name Dvorak, without rolling the *r* too much.

The Chinese make only a few exceptions in their new romanization of Chinese words: Sun Yat-sen, China, and Confucius remain the same. But most familiar people and places now look quite different, even Peking and Mao Tse-tung. Here is a list of common new spellings with the old ones to the right.

Pinyin	Wade-Giles
women	**women**
Ban Zhao	Pan Chao
Ci Xi	Tz'u Hsi
Deng Yingshao	Teng Ying-chao
Ding Ling	Ting Ling
Guan Yin	Kuan-Yin
Jiang Qing	Chiang Ch'ing
Song Meiling	Soong May-ling
Song Qinling	Soong Ching-ling
men	**men**
Deng Xiaoping	Teng Hsiao-ping
Hua Guofeng	Hua Kuo-feng
Mao Zedong	Mao Tse-tung
Zhou Enlai	Chou En-lai
place names:	**place names:**
Beijing	Peking
Chongqing	Chungking
Guangzhou	Canton
Tianjin	Tientsin